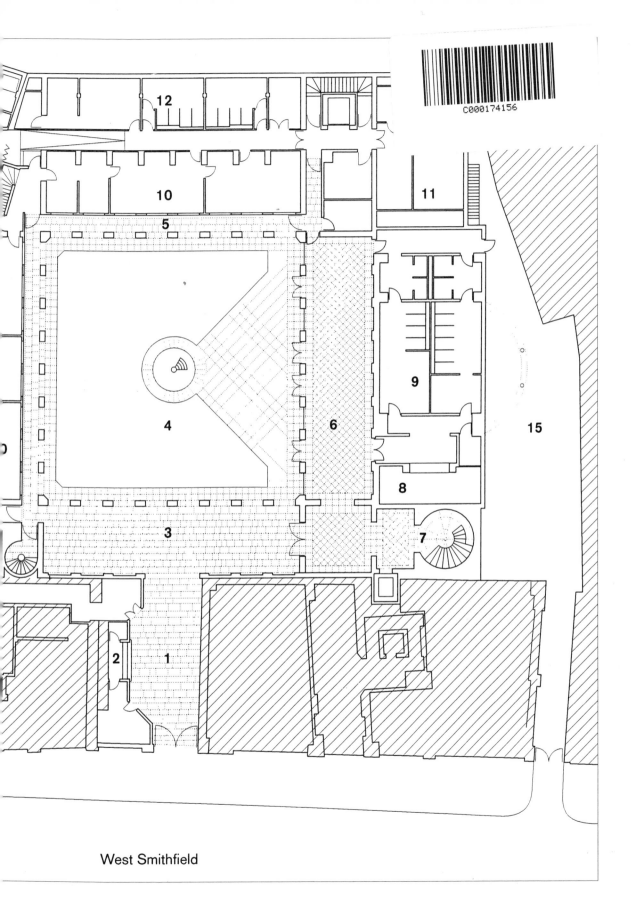

12

10

5

11

9

4

6

15

8

3

7

2   1

West Smithfield

THE HABERDASHERS' COMPANY

IN THE LATER TWENTIETH CENTURY

Her Majesty The Queen opens the new Hall, West Smithfield, 24 October 2002.

THE HABERDASHERS' COMPANY

IN THE LATER TWENTIETH CENTURY

Ian W. Archer

Phillimore

2004

Published by
PHILLIMORE & CO. LTD
Shopwyke Manor Barn, Chichester, West Sussex, England

ISBN 1 86077 318 4

Printed and bound in Great Britain by
CAMBRIDGE PRINTING

Contents

List of Illustrations

Frontispiece: HM The Queen opens the new Hall, West Smithfield, 24 October 2002

Foreword

In 1991, the Haberdashers' Company published a comprehensive history of the Company from its origins in the 14th century to the latter half of the 20th century. The author, Dr Ian Archer, produced a lively and fascinating account of the Company's progress through the centuries. However by necessity, the last chapter relating to the second half of the 20th century was brief in comparison to the earlier part of the book.

In this new history, Dr Archer has paid special attention to this latter period during which considerable change to the Company's fortunes took place together with significant progress in the educational side of the Company's activities. Furthermore, the post-war Hall, built in 1956 at the side of Garrard House in Gresham Street, on a site acquired on 24 September 1458, was demolished out of necessity. A new site was acquired in West Smithfield from the trustees of Saint Bartholomew's Hospital on which a new Hall was constructed to the design by Sir Michael Hopkins and Partners and opened in 2002.

The company hopes that readers will find this additional history of the Company as lively and interesting as the first. The Company joins with the author in thanking those who have contributed to this book so magnificently.

JULIEN PREVETT
Master

5 October 2004

Acknowledgements

It is 13 years since my original *History of the Haberdashers' Company* was completed in 1991. I was honoured at that time with the freedom of the Company. Since then I have enjoyed the Company's hospitality, learned more about its activities, cemented many existing friendships, and fostered new ones. The spirit of fraternity (the starting point for any historian of early modern guilds such as myself) remains very much alive.

I was therefore pleased to accept the Company's request for an up-date to the original *History* covering the period from the Second World War. During that period the Company has seen one Hall destroyed by enemy action, and another removed by the developers' cranes, and it has moved its location from the historic Staining Lane site to West Smithfield where an exciting new Hall has been built. The years after the war also witnessed a remarkable financial recovery which has sustained a more vigorous corporate life and enabled the Company to diversify its charitable activities.

In writing this supplementary volume I have been fortunate indeed in being able to draw upon the wisdom of two of the original members of the History Committee of the later 1980s, Past Master Brian Shawcross and the former Clerk to the Company, Captain Michael Barrow. They have managed just the right mixture of encouragement and criticism to nudge the project along and to refine and clarify the argument. Captain Barrow, unsparing though he might be with the red pen, has nevertheless answered countless enquiries, and provided crucial illustrative material. John Cope, the Company's Archivist, has also been a member of the Steering Committee. Much of the research for the project took place at a time when access to the archives was difficult because of the Company's temporary accommodation in 39/40 Bartholomew Close, but John did his best to make the work run smoothly. He has also been a mine of information about the Company's art, and he has provided invaluable assistance with the illustrations. His predecessor as Archivist, Helen Bradley, worked on the original *History*, and the research notes she took then have been as useful to this project as the previous one. Noel Osborne of Phillimore provides another bridge between the original *History* and the present volume. He has continued to provide sagacious advice.

Among those who have been interviewed, I would like to single out Sir Brian Jenks, Harold Quitman, and Christopher Bostock. Not only did they provide critical insights, but they have read and commented helpfully on early drafts. Christopher Bostock also let me read his fascinating blow-by-blow account of the Hatcham CTC project. Others who have been interviewed include Gordon Bourne, Bruce McGowan, Anthony Miller, Mark Powell, David Sime, Graeme

Walker, Sir John Welch, and Michael Wheldon. Other members have answered specific enquiries: among them Donald Adamson, Christopher Maunder-Taylor, Julien Prevett, and Neil Stratford. David and Ruth Taylor generously allowed me to read their exemplary *Mr Adams' Free Grammar School* in advance of its publication. Keith Way and Philip Edwards read the chapters on finance and on the new Hall, and they are much improved for their interventions.

One of the pleasures of writing the History has been the opportunity to get to know the Company staff. They have not only answered a stream of ill-informed enquiries, but they have frequently had me perched on the edge of their desks. I am very grateful to Brian Blair, Peter Eaglestone, David Evans, Michael Kerrigan, Helen Marlow, Tim Marsh, and Eddie O'Shea. They have made researching the book a truly convivial experience. The Clerk, Captain Robert Fisher, has kept a benevolent eye on progress, and helpfully ironed out solecisms and error at a late stage.

The original *History* was written during my five-year sojourn in Cambridge. I have since returned to Oxford, and I am fortunate in the support my College and Faculty have offered me. Most of the archival spade work for this book was done during a period of sabbatical leave at the end of 2001. The Bodleian Library has provided essential secondary materials, and I am often left wondering where I would have been without the electronic resources mounted on its OXLIP platform. I have as always received a warm and helpful welcome from the Guildhall Library in London. Lewisham Local Studies Library provided additional materials.

The 'later twentieth century' is emphatically not 'my period', but an early modern historian can nevertheless feel at home with the study of a Livery Company, for there are many continuities, both in structures of governance and in ethos. What makes a modern Livery Company interesting, though, is the way in which the tensions between tradition and modernity are negotiated. That provides a major theme for the present work.

IAN W. ARCHER
Keble College, Oxford

March 2004

Notes on Sources

The bulk of the research material for this book lies in the Company's own archive. The minutes of the Company's courts and committees before 1980 are kept at the Guildhall Library, but access to the more recent volumes stored there requires the Company's permission. Minutes of the years after 1980 are at the time of writing kept at the Hall.

List of Abbreviations

AAAC	Aske and Adams Advisory Committee
CA	Court of Assistants
CC	Charities Committee
CW	Court of Wardens
EC	Estates Committee
EdC	Education Committee
ESC	Estates Sub-Committee
EScC	Endowed Schools Committee
FAC	Fine Arts Committee
FC	Finance Committee
GL	Guildhall Library
HAACAC	Haberdashers' Aske's and Adams Charities Advisory Committee
HACC	Haberdashers' Aske's Charity Committee
JMAC	Jones' Monmouth Advisory Committee
JMCC	Jones' Monmouth Charities Committee
OCC	Officers' and Clerk's Committee
PC	Property Committee
SC	Schools Committee

Chapter One

The Company in the Second World War

The Luftwaffe raid on the city of London on the night of Sunday 29 December 1940 was by no means the largest assault on the capital during the Blitz, but it was the most damaging. There was a strong westerly wind which assisted the spread of fires, and the Thames was low which hindered the efforts of the fire-fighters to get access to water. Moreover, many city buildings were not being properly watched. At Haberdashers' Hall, however, Mr A.E.V. Hooke, the acting under-Beadle, was on duty with three men (actually in excess of the normal roster of two), while in the basement Mr Shrimpton, the A.R.P. Warden, was at his post. As fires started in the vicinity of the Hall Hooke phoned Mr Davis, the acting Beadle, who rushed to Staining Lane from his house at Beckenham. The scene which greeted him was appalling. Incendiary bombs had fallen at the corner of Noble Street, the fires spreading rapidly to the empty buildings surrounding. Hooke (who suffered an injury to his eye) and his team struggled hard to prevent the fires spreading to the Hall, but then a high explosive bomb hit the back of the Hall. The sprinklers only operated for a few minutes before the water supply failed (the main had been severed), and in spite of all Davis' entreaties, the firemen dealing with fires on the south side of Gresham Street were unable to run a hose to Staining Lane. Within a few minutes the fire had engulfed the Hall. Realising there was now no way of saving the building, Davis and his men began efforts to salvage what they could. As they were emptying the contents of the cigar cabinet, the roof of the Master's flat fell in, and they were lucky to escape with their lives.[1]

At the end of the 'second great fire of London' the Hall and the surrounding company properties (31 and 35-45 Staining Lane, leased to Taplings, 4 Staining Lane leased to Dent, Allcroft and Sons, and 105-107 Wood Street leased to United Kingdom Property Co.) had been reduced to rubble.[2] The losses would have been greater still had the Company not taken the precaution before the outbreak of the war of moving its pictures, the Master's chair, and the barge figurehead of St Catherine to Monmouth Boys' School, and its plate to the vaults of the Bank of England and Lloyds at Monmouth.[3] Although the wine in the outer cellar had been lost as a door had collapsed, that in the inner cellar was largely undamaged, and the Company had taken the precaution of removing its brandy to the cellar of the Headmaster of Monmouth School.[4]

The destruction of the Hall was a calamity, but it was only one of numerous problems created for the Company by the war, which had an immediate impact on the Company's finances. Taxation rose steeply, quarterage receipts and other dues from members declined, and payments in management charges from the charities (calculated as a percentage of gross rents) fell. Although there were

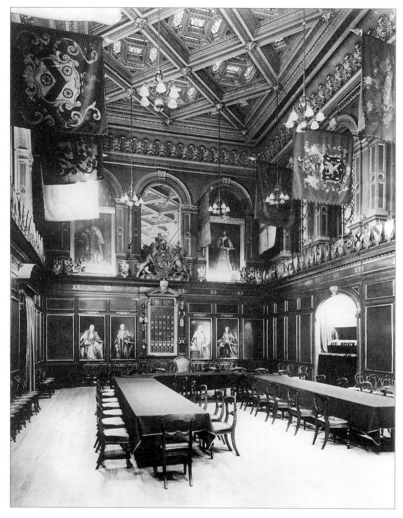

1 Interior of the Livery Hall before the Second World War.

savings on entertainments and on attendance fees, there were additional costs such as the renting of office space at Chislehurst near the Clerk's house, to which the staff had been evacuated on the outbreak of war.[5] The situation radically deteriorated with the damage to corporate properties in the Blitz. The Company was determined not to let its ground rents fall into abeyance, but this was undermined by revisions to the legislation in 1941 which allowed lessees of ground-rented war-damaged property to disclaim their leases. By the end of the war the rents on disclaimed properties amounted to £3,945 per annum (approximately one quarter of the total rents receivable on the corporate account).[6] There was an unfortunate messy wrangle with Thomas Tapling & Co.,

2 View of the war-damaged Hall after the bombing of 29 December
1940, showing the arcading.

the lessees of the valuable property in Gresham Street and Staining Lane
adjacent to the Hall, arising from a near-fatal misunderstanding of what had
happened at a meeting on 20 February between the Company's advisers and
Lord Cottesloe and the representatives of Taplings. Taplings had wanted to
postpone the payment of their sixth premium of £2,500 due on their lease in
June 1941 pending a clarification of the position with respect to the replanning
of the City which would enable the parties to decide about the possibility of a
reversionary lease. Taplings insisted that the Haberdashers had agreed to this
proposal; however, Major E.A. Dodd (Livery, 1895), the Master, was adamant
that they had not. The parties came close to litigation, but eventually agreed
in 1943 to split the difference between Taplings' offer and the Haberdasher
demands for a lump sum for cancellation of the contract.[7]

Although initial projections had suggested that the deficit could be contained
to £250 in 1939-40, by June 1940 the corporate accounts were heading for
a deficit of £1,900. Sir Maurice Jenks (Master, 1941) can perhaps be forgiven
for his motion that, at the height of the Battle of Britain, the present critical
situation was no time to look into the details of balancing the budget.[8] There
was some reluctance, however, to confront the harsh realities of war. An obvious
target for cuts was the fees paid to Court members, but there was considerable
pressure to continue them as, in the words of a special committee of February
1941, 'the burden placed on those responsible for the management of the
Company is great, and for the benefit of posterity and worthy of recognition'.

3 View of the war-damaged area north of St Paul's Cathedral, painting by Charles Cundall, 1956 (Luncheon Room, Haberdashers' Hall.).

The Special Committee in September 1941 recommended no further economies in spite of an anticipated deficit of £1,500 for 1940-1. At the subsequent Court of Assistants, an accountant C.E. Fletcher (Livery, 1901, Master, 1945) pointed out that, without real cuts in expenditure, the Company's liquid assets would be used up within twenty years. To his suggestion that expenditure on Court fees, lunches, and cigars could be cut further, Jenks responded that the position of the Haberdashers was completely different from that of a limited liability company with responsibilities to shareholders. In an interesting statement of the constitutional position he reminded the Court that they were under no obligation to the Livery to cut expenditure, and therefore they were justified in overspending on gifts and lunches.[9]

   The Company's reluctance to cut expenditure may be explained by the sacrifices it was already making. At the outset of the war it had been decided that no Livery Dinners could be held, and economies were applied to Court lunches by abandoning the sweet. It was proposed that the Banks Dinner to which the ladies of the Court were invited should be replaced by a lunch, but in the event it had to be cancelled because of the Battle of Britain, and there was no lunch in 1941 because of the financial situation. A projected lunch for some of the Livery in 1940 met the same fate. Deputations to the Company schools were scaled back to include only the Master, First Warden, and the Company's representatives on the schools' governing bodies.[10] The vote of thanks to R.L. Carter (Livery, 1894, Master, 1939) at the close of his year as Master in November 1940 noted that he had held office in trying times without the compensation of hosting 'pleasant entertainments' in the Hall.[11] Assistants continued to sit down to lunches after their meetings, but they were encouraged to drink beer, and were soon confined to one glass of wine.[12] The number of meetings of the Court of Assistants was cut to ten in 1940, and to seven in 1941 to save on attendance fees and lunches.[13]

It was perhaps ironic that it was during Jenks' Mastership in 1941-2 that more serious attempts at economy were made. By March 1942 the accumulated wartime deficit on the corporate account stood at £7,234. The Special Committee on finances recommended that lunches become sandwich affairs with no soup; that Court gifts be cut from three guineas to two guineas, and gifts to the Banks trustees from four guineas to three guineas; that wines be sold to raise between £750 and £1,000, and that the number of committee meetings be curtailed. The Second Warden, the stockbroker, Reymond Powell (Livery, 1896, Master, 1943), pressed for still more radical measures, including a cut in Court meetings to four, and a move of the offices back from Kent to New Cross. In the event the original proposals were carried: sandwich lunches were to cost no more than 4s. 6d. per head, and there was to be no service. Livery entertainments remained in abeyance.[14] A major structural review was also carried out in 1942; the sub-committees of the Estates, Finance, and Charities Committees were abolished and their work transferred to the relevant parent committee; the size of these standing committees was limited to eight members each, and the Endowed Schools Committee was fixed at eleven. These were considered to be wartime emergency measures and were to be subject to annual review.[15] Another innovation (strongly pressed by Charles Fletcher, one of the accountants on the Court) was the appointment of professional auditors for the first time, although in an interesting demonstration of the working of city networks and in what would nowadays be regarded as a conflict of interest, it was agreed to approach Mr Prince, the partner of James Gibson Harris (Livery, 1899), to do the work.[16] The combined effect of the economies and tighter financial control was that there was some reduction in the deficit on the corporate account from £1,652 in 1941-2 to £993 in 1942-3.[17]

Powell's suggestion of locating the offices in New Cross was not followed up, but the principle of a move back to London was accepted. The Company's meetings after the destruction of the Hall were held at Grocers' Hall, at a cost of £350 per annum, but although the Haberdashers were grateful for their 'courteous and ready hospitality', there were serious problems of office space.[18] By the spring of 1942 as the raids on London had ceased, it was realised that the offices could be moved from Chislehurst in Kent to save money if suitable accommodation could be found. The Vintners offered the Haberdashers the lease of a floor of their Hall complex, and they moved in in September 1942. The savings from the move were estimated at £600 per annum. It was the start of a long association, for the Haberdashers remained at 1, Vintners' Place until the opening of their new Hall in 1956.[19]

There is something rather impressive about the dogged determination with which the Company attempted to maintain its routines in extremely trying conditions. It was difficult to recruit new blood on to the Court of Assistants because of war service by many of the Livery, and there were interminable discussions about the appropriate size of the Court, and in turn whether the Junior Wardens should be recruited directly from the Livery.[20] Nevertheless, the Company adhered firmly to constitutional principle so that a proposal in October 1940 that an emergency executive committee consisting of the Master, Wardens, and designated Court members should deal with business in place of the standing committees was thrown out. Although it was clearly difficult to secure full attendance, members did struggle in through the war-torn city.[21] On 23 January 1941, for example, the Master commended the three senior past Masters who had made long journeys from the country to attend a meeting of the Charities Sub-committee.[22] There are various touching signs of the effort to maintain continuities: at a Court of Wardens meeting on 4 March 1941 the Wardens authorised the purchase of a new hamper to carry wine to deputations, and the reprinting of the *Sure Guide*, a moralistic tract directed to new apprentices, the Company's stock of which had been destroyed in the bombing of the Hall.[23] There was a strong sense of the importance of maintaining the archives. The records had been microfilmed on the eve of the war: when the microfilms were destroyed, the Company arranged for their re-microfilming, and the storage of the new films in the vaults of Lloyds Bank at Monmouth. Water-damaged records, including the earliest minute books, were salvaged from the ruined Hall, and repaired by the staff of the Public Records Office.[24] Likewise, the ceremonial paraphernalia of the Company was maintained: the garlands of the Master and Wardens, damaged beyond repair in the fire, were replaced at a cost of £14 12s. 0d.; the medals fortunately had survived.[25] The Company maintained its dignified observances. As the first Blitz drew to a close members of the Court assembled in their gowns in the crypt of the miraculously preserved St Paul's Cathedral on 12 May 1941 to attend a memorial service for Alderman Sir George Wyatt Truscott, Lord Mayor in 1908, and Master in 1911-12.[26]

The Company's schools felt the pressures of war directly. On its outbreak the pupils of the Aske schools were evacuated from London. The Hatcham boys went to Oxted in Kent and the girls initially to Hove on the south coast and after one term to Teignmouth in South Devon, finally moving to Barnstaple in 1942.[27] The Acton girls were at Dorchester (Dorset) for a few months during the phoney war.[28] There were considerable tensions between the evacuees and their hosts. The Dorchester locals were outraged by the London parents coming on motorised jaunts from London to visit their Acton daughters while not contributing to their keep. One old Askean described Oxted as a 'smug dormitory town in the stockbroker belt full of landowners and retired generals and assize judges'. Some of the locals on whom the pupils were billeted, and under delusions about the wealth of the Company, wanted additional allowances, and had to be tactfully informed of the true

4 Evacuated pupils from Acton Girls' School with the Bishop of Salisbury at Fordington St George, St Catherine's Day, 1939.

state of affairs by the Clerk and Master of the Company who met with the Billeting Officers. Ned Goddard, the Headmaster from 1932 to 1961, had to use all his diplomatic skills in keeping the peace with his resentful opposite number at Oxted County School, where the Haberdashers were taught before moving to two large houses at Limpsfield.[29] When the V1 flying bomb attacks began in 1944, Oxted was considered unsafe and there was another move to Teignmouth.[30] The Newport, Bunbury, and Monmouth schools by contrast received evacuees from elsewhere. The Adams Grammar School at Newport in Shropshire took in 294 boys from Holly Lodge School in the Smethwick district of Birmingham, adjusting its timetable so that the evacuees were taught in the afternoon and evenings, and the locals in the mornings, including Saturdays. Monmouth received evacuees from the West Midlands, taking in pupils from King Edward's Grammar School, Birmingham. Bunbury took in 55 pupils from Liverpool. These evacuation arrangements were somewhat partial: many of the Smethwick and Liverpool boys returned home after a few months, many of the London pupils (particularly those from Acton and Hampstead) drifted

5 Old school buildings at Bunbury.

back to the emergency schools in the capital. The schools, however, retained their mixed character: Bunbury in January 1941 had 55 Cheshire children, 20 Liverpool evacuees, and 14 Guernsey evacuees.[31]

The war also brought a halt to building projects: the planned expansion of facilities at Newport was one of the first casualties.[32] The vacated buildings of the London schools were targeted by the local authority for wartime administrative needs. Thus the upper floor of the Hatcham Girls' School was occupied by the Deptford Borough Council for the management of its food supply.[33] There was also extensive bomb damage to the London schools. At Hatcham the upper floors of the Girls' School suffered minor damage, but at the Boys' School there was direct damage to the common room and dining hall on 29 December 1940, the same night that the Hall had been consumed, and an incendiary bomb had hit the library.[34] Still worse hit were the north London schools. A direct hit on Acton Girls' School in October 1940 destroyed the Prosser Library and the dining room in the west wing.[35] Whereas at Hatcham Boys the Blitz damage was estimated at £2,305, at Hampstead Boys it was £12,080, and at Acton Girls at £18,120.[36] Even Monmouth, which was on the Luftwaffe route to the West Midlands, had several bombs dropped on its playing fields, and the upper dormitories were vacated as a precautionary measure.[37]

The schools were also seriously threatened by the undermining of their financial base, as the income from the charities underpinning them fell. The bulk of the income for the Aske and Jones foundations came from estates in Hoxton (Shoreditch) and New Cross respectively. These estates had been attached to the charities by their 17th-century donors; they had been rural in nature, but in the 19th century they had undergone residential development and

6 South front of Acton Girls' School from Creffield Road.

their value had appreciated substantially. However, as metropolitan residential estates, they were vulnerable in wartime. Pressure to reduce rents was felt from the outbreak of hostilities. The Company, mindful of the effects on the income of the charity, was reluctant to do this, although it was prepared to accept surrenders of leases, and it offered some reductions in the case of businesses whose presence was desirable. By 1942 it was evident that a more liberal policy was necessary, and it became common to offer reductions in rent of 25 per cent.[38] The war had a more direct impact on charity income in the destruction of estate property through bombing. The Blitz on London commenced on 7 September 1940, and the capital was bombed every night until 2 November, intermittently thereafter. By early October it was evident that both the New Cross and Hoxton estates had been hard hit.[39] But worse was to follow. On 8 December the Hoxton estate was devastated by a parachute mine. What was particularly depressing was that the recently constructed flats were severely damaged: Fanshawe House was almost completely destroyed, and one third of Aske House became uninhabitable. The Company's surveyor estimated the damage on that single night to have been £80,000, and that the net loss of income to the charity would be £4,000-5,000 per annum.[40] Although the raids ended on the night of 12-13 May 1941, there was a recurrence of the agony in the closing year of the war, as Hitler launched his 'pilotless planes', flying bombs (the 'doodlebugs') on the city. Between 13 June and 1 September 1944 2,340 V1 flying bombs fell on London, followed by another 517 still more powerful and deadly (because almost impossible to shoot down) V2 rockets between 8 September 1944 and 27 March 1945. The Hatcham estate was hit particularly hard by the new attacks. The Woolworth's store on the New Cross

7 Monmouth Grammar School for Boys, showing the Gateway.

Road which crossed the estate was the scene of the worst V2 disaster with 168 fatalities on 29 November. Already by 18 July 1944, 71 houses had been demolished, 99 badly damaged (some needing demolition), and another 409 had undergone medium damage. By the end of the year 186 houses with a market value of over £100,000 had been destroyed at Hatcham and 83 houses with a market value of over £28,000 at Hoxton.[41]

The few rural properties were also adversely affected by the war. At both Knighton in Shropshire (a property supporting the Adams school at Newport) and Singleton in Kent (the income from which was largely allocated to the Aske charity) grassland was ploughed up for tillage to maximise food output. Shortage of timber resulted in pressure from the Ministry of Supply for access to the Knighton woods.[42] Singleton suffered still worse from the attentions of the military; it was used as a billet for troops in the preparations against invasion in 1940; its lawns were wrecked by trenches, its woods damaged by training exercises. In 1943 parts of the Kent estate were requisitioned by the Air Ministry for landing fields at Kingsnorth and Great Chart as well as a P.O.W. camp.[43]

8 Original buildings at Haberdashers' Monmouth Girls' School.

The result of the deterioration in the Company's estates had a direct effect on the charities. The most serious problems were faced by the Aske Schools. In 1940 the net income of the Estates Governors had been £13,500; in 1941 it fell to approximately £7,000.[44] The Governors' freedom of manoeuvre was constrained by the terms of the 1927 agreement with the London County Council (L.C.C.) that the fixed sum of £4,946 per annum should go to the Hatcham schools, meaning that the financial squeeze was felt directly by the north London schools at Hampstead and Acton. By early 1942 the financial situation of the northern schools was dire. Their bank overdraft stood at £7,000 and was expected to increase by £7,000 per annum; Barclays Bank was pressing for some further security. The School Governors were given a roasting by Sir Maurice Jenks for not having taken adequate counter-measures, but the situation had deteriorated rapidly, and staff could not simply be laid off without notice. An application was made to the London County Council for a revision to the 1927 agreement, while an approach was made to the Board of Education for further assistance for the Acton and Hampstead Schools. Closure was seriously contemplated: on 24 February 1942 the School Governors had agreed to closure with effect from the end of the summer term, and this was confirmed by the Estates Governors on 4 March. In the event the schools were saved from closure. Fees were increased to bring in an extra £4,500 per annum; the Board of Education promised to make a sizeable contribution to the northern schools in proportion to the loss in estate income, and the L.C.C. agreed to revise the 1927 scheme, so that the Hatcham and northern schools could receive the estate income in proportions determined by the number of pupils at the schools.[45]

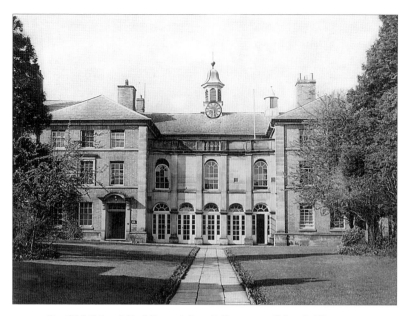

9 Old School Building, Adams' Grammar School, Newport.

The Company's discretionary charitable activity was also severely curtailed by the war, as there were insufficient corporate resources to sustain an adequate programme of giving. At an early stage it had been decided to refer all appeals direct to the Finance Committee, rather than having them considered by the Charities Committee.[46] Many worthy wartime appeals had to be turned down, but important obligations like the £25 per annum paid to the P.O.W. fund of the Company's adopted regiment, the Queen Victoria Rifles (many had been part of the British Expeditionary Force and captured at Dunkirk) were maintained.[47] The fall in charitable income affected the minor charities too. By early 1941 the Company was forced into the expedient of selling investments representing unused accumulations of income. This was seen as preferable to cutting pensions, but it meant that the capital base of the charities was further eroded.[48]

It was one of the striking features of the Second World War that even in the depths of conflict, creative thinking about the country's future was underway. The Haberdashers had declared in the dark days of 1941 that they would rebuild their Hall as near as possible to its ancient site.[49] But what would be the shape of the City that would rise from the rubble? In what ways would the City have to adapt to modern needs, for example those of motor transport? How far would opportunities be taken in the damaged housing estates to improve amenities? How centrally directed would redevelopment be? How would priorities for reconstruction be determined? These were questions which posed challenges as well as opportunities to the Haberdashers. It was characteristic of the lack of a properly integrated approach to London that separate plans emerged for the City, County, and Greater London.[50]

10   Haberdashers' Aske's School, Hampstead, main buildings.

In early 1943, at the instigation of the Bank of England, the City of London Reconstruction Advisory Committee was set up, representing the interests of key city institutions like the Bank, the accepting houses, and the Livery Companies. Its aim was to act as a channel through which the planning authorities could get advice from city bodies. As the City's plan emerged, the Haberdashers attempted to co-ordinate their responses with those of the other Great Twelve Companies, and early in 1945 they set up a special committee of seven under the chairmanship of the architect and engineer F.E. Tudor (Livery, 1901, Master, 1946, at this time Second Warden) to deal with the war damages claims and rebuilding of the Hall and the city properties.[51]

Signs of future tensions were evident in the Company's response to the L.C.C.'s plans for the Hoxton and Hatcham estates in 1944. There were disagreements as to priorities: on the East Road of the Hoxton estate the Council scheme showed housing in place of run-down shops; the Company Surveyor thought light industry more appropriate. Likewise, the northern part of the Hatcham estate which had suffered considerable damage through subsidence should be redesignated for industrial use, especially in view of the railways surrounding. There were also potential threats to estate income. The council scheme for Hoxton included a Civic Centre on Aske Sreet and Ashford Street: as it would involve compulsory purchase, the charity faced the likelihood of a permanent cut in income. Nothing of course was yet decided, but it was clear that

11   Haberdashers' Aske's Boys' School, Hatcham, old building.

reconstruction was going to involve a great deal of delicate negotiation with bodies enjoying greater clout than the Company.[52] It was a sign of things to come that the Company was forced into the rebuilding of the Aske House flats in 1944 to pre-empt a requisitioning by the local authority. On the Hatcham estate the Company was annoyed by the L.C.C.'s requisitioning of vacant sites for prefabricated housing. Some of the 'prefabs', as they were called, were still in existence in the 1980s.[53]

The other major challenge to the Company came in the field of educational reform. There were attempts by the L.C.C. aided schools to affect the course of the legislation. At the end of 1943 the Association of London Aided Schools was formed to encourage co-operation between the governing bodies of the schools and to work to safeguard their position. F.E. Tudor was a member of its executive committee and was involved in lobbying the Minister of Education, R.A. Butler, early in 1944, as the provisions of his Education Bill were unveiled, with a view to securing provisions to protect the independence of the governing bodies.[54] For those schools with sufficient endowment the direct grant option could be followed. This would involve a fee-paying school receiving an annual grant direct from the Ministry of £29 per pupil over the age of 11 in return for an allocation of 25 per cent of the annual entry in free places which were to be taken up by the L.E.A. or (should the L.E.A. decline) by pupils already in the schools. For less well endowed schools there were basically two options under which the schools would form part of the

12   Haberdashers' Aske's Girls' School, Hatcham, old building.

L.E.A. system of free education while the Company could still enjoy a say in their running. If the Governors were able and willing to pay one half of the cost of improvements and alterations to school buildings, they could apply for voluntary aided status, by which the Governors would continue to appoint teachers. If the endowments could not support 50 per cent of building and maintenance costs, then the Governors could apply for voluntary controlled status, by which the L.E.A. took over responsibility for the maintenance of the schools and nominated half the Governors.[55]

When the provisions of the 1944 act were considered by the Haberdashers' Endowed Schools Committee in October 1944, the Company considered a fourth option for its less well endowed schools. In pursuing the aim of maximising the benefit for its most prestigious schools, it proposed to follow the direct grant option for the Aske schools at Acton and Hampstead and the Jones schools at Monmouth, while transferring to the local authority lock, stock, and barrel the Hatcham schools and the West Monmouthshire School on condition that the whole of the income of the respective charities could be applied to the direct grant schools. Newport was a different case because

13 Guy Eagleton,
Clerk to the Company (1931-50).

there was no other school supported by the charity which could benefit from the terms of such a transfer. The discussion recorded in the minutes is quite revealing about the Company's priorities. F.E. Tudor and Sir Gerald Wollaston (Livery, 1896, Master, 1942) stressed the need to secure schools as free from outside control as possible because those coming under the government's scheme voluntarily would sooner or later become part of the national system of education and lose their special character; it was better to have four schools on a completely independent basis than eight under partial control.[56] (Ned Goddard, Headmaster of Hatcham Boys since 1932, recalls in his memoirs how astonished he was when, on his appointment, the Clerk Guy Eagleton had opined that the Company would be better off if it could dispose of the Hatcham Schools 'lock, stock, and barrel'.)[57] Those issues of control and the preservation of the schools' special character were to define the Company's relationship with the schools for the rest of the century.

So, as the war came to an end, the Haberdashers' Company existed on a precarious financial basis. Its Hall and many of the corporate properties had been destroyed. The social life of the Company was considerably diminished. The capital base of its core charities had been eroded. Its schools faced an uncertain future in a post-war world of increasing state regulation. Its capacity to regenerate its finances was reduced by the weakness of its resources and the planners' constraints. Reconstruction of the Company's charitable work and corporate life was going to be a long haul.

Chapter Two

Financial Transformations

In discussing the financial fortunes of the Haberdashers in the later 20th century, it is important to reiterate at the outset the very clear distinction between charitable and corporate resources. It is a distinction which is sometimes lost in the public perception of Livery Companies which is distorted by their social round. The funds supporting the social activities of the Haberdashers' Company are non-charitable and totally separate from the charitable funds of which the Company is trustee, the accounts of which are received by the Charity Commissioners. The Company levies a management charge on the charities at a level which must be approved by the Charity Commission. It is also relevant that in addition to managing the trusts imposed on it by the terms of donors' wills, the Company makes contributions from its corporate funds to charities. The distinction between corporate and trust monies is fundamental to the Company's financial management and accountancy procedures, and will be maintained in the discussion which follows.

The key charities were those of Robert Aske and William Jones, both of which were still based on estates they had acquired in the 17th century. From William Jones' bequest in 1613 the Company had acquired the manor of Hatcham Barnes in what is now the New Cross area of south-east London. The bequest of the silk merchant Robert Aske in 1690 had been used to purchase an estate in Hoxton in north London as well as a number of rural properties a few miles from Ashford in Kent. Both the Hoxton and Hatcham estates had been rural in nature at the time when they were acquired by the Company in trust, but the expansion of the metropolis meant that they had been developed in the 19th century. Hoxton's development came first with much building concentrated on the years around 1800; the development of Hatcham was a later 19th century phenomenon, commencing after the demolition of the manor house formerly occupied by the Hardcastle family in 1869, and undertaken mainly by William Snooke, the Company's Surveyor between 1875 and 1900. By 1940 the Hoxton estate comprised 21 acres, with houses on both sides of Pitfield Street, the eastern side of East Road, Styman Street, Great Chart Street, Haberdasher Street, Bevenden Street, Singleton Street, Baches Street, the south side of Pimlico Walk, Kingsnorth Place, Aske Street, Fanshaw Street, Ashford Street, and Short Street. The Hatcham estate originally comprised 323 acres, but portions had been sold to railway companies in the 19th century. It was bisected by the New Cross Road, to the north of which the Company had built small terraced houses, while to the south (as in Pepys Road built in the 1880s) they had constructed semi-detached houses for more prosperous people. The poorer relation was the Adams foundation of William Adams (1656) which

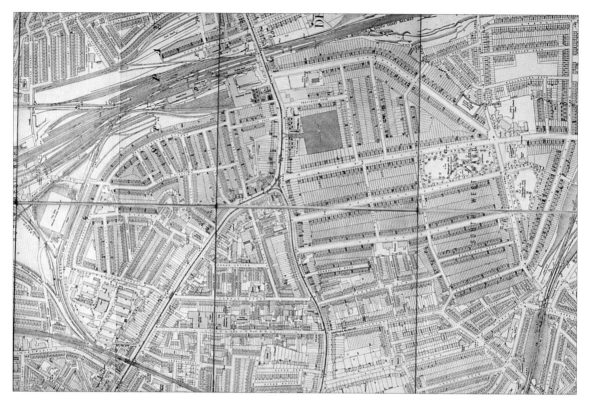

14   Detail of map of Hatcham (New Cross) estate, 1931.

supported the school at Newport in Shropshire. The charity estate at Knighton comprised 911 acres (806 of which were assigned to Adams' and 105 to Jones' charity). This was primarily agricultural land, though it also included some woodland and a milk condensing plant owned by Cadburys.[1]

As we saw in the first chapter, the war had left the Company's estates at Hatcham and Hoxton in a parlous position. Both had suffered substantial war damage; of the many vacant sites several had been requisitioned for emergency pre-fabricated housing by the L.C.C. or the local Deptford and Shoreditch Borough Councils. On the Hoxton estate redevelopment had commenced before the war with the construction of several blocks of flats, but these too had been damaged. At Hatcham a large number of ground-rent leases were due to fall in, making redevelopment a pressing priority. Immediately after the war, however, the rebuilding funds of the two estates were very low: at Hatcham rebuilding costs alone (let alone any more extensive redevelopment) were estimated at £100,000, and in 1946 the rebuilding fund stood at only £8,965 5s. 4d. It became a matter of urgent priority to put aside the maximum amounts possible from estate income to build up these funds, however tight the constraints on school income might become.[2]

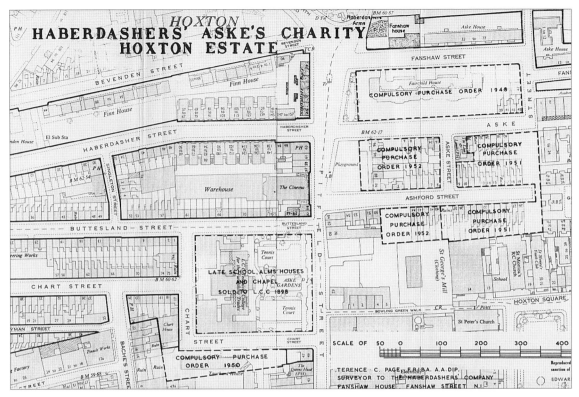

15   Map of Hoxton estate, showing effects of post-war compulsory purchase orders.

The immediate post-war years were intensely frustrating as the Company had to steer a perilous course through the constraints set by its own limited financial resources, the tight control over all post-war construction, and the planning powers of the L.C.C. and the local boroughs, backed by their compulsory purchase powers. In 1947, for example, the Company negotiated with the L.C.C. and Shoreditch Borough Council, and gained approval for the redevelopment of Fanshawe Street. The scheme involved several five-storey blocks of 160 flats at a total estimated cost of £174,000, towards which a value payment of £29,000 from the War Damage Commission was due; there was some compensation from the L.C.C. for land needed for the extension of St Monica's Roman Catholic school, but the project still required £145,000 in financing. The anticipated net rents would be £4,320 (that is 60 per cent of gross receipts), representing a return of 4.5 per cent on net outlay, a very small margin if the redevelopment were to be financed by loans. The Company considered setting the charity up as a Housing Association under the Housing Act of 1936, qualifying it for loans from the L.C.C. repayable over 60 years. Unfortunately the Charitable Trusts Act forbade loans to charities over longer terms than 30 years, and the repayments on a 30-year loan would not leave a sufficient surplus for the

16 Properties on the Hatcham estate: (i) New Cross Gate, Victorian residential properties; (ii) Waller Road, Victorian residential properties; (iii) Avignon Road flats, post-war residential developments; (iv) Blundell House (1964), post-war commercial developments.

schools. It was clearly an extremely risky undertaking especially in view of the low anticipated return (as the flats would be subject to rent control), and in July 1948 the Estates Committee recommended abandonment of the scheme, and the sale of the site to the L.C.C. It was hoped that part of the surveyors' and architects' fees could be recovered from the council, but the Company's position was weak as the compulsory purchase order had come a full four months after the Company's decision to abandon its scheme. In the event, no compensation for the charity's lost expenditure was received.[3]

1948 also proved to be a crunch year at Hatcham. The Company had come up with a plan for the development of flats on Avignon Road, but this was blocked by Aneurin Bevan, the Minister of Health. At the same time Deptford Council was pursuing compulsory purchase orders on properties on New Cross Road, Goodwood Road, Erlanger Road, and Waller Road irrespective of the Haberdashers' plans. The Company attempted to outflank Deptford by putting its own proposals to the L.C.C., but the latter was unsympathetic, and the Minister of Health was expected to support the local authority. The Estate Governors recognised that the loss of properties on the periphery of the estate

17 Properties on the Hoxton estate: (i) *Prince of Wales* public house; (ii) Aske House flats; (iii) 'London Maid' commercial premises. (iv) Haberdasher Street flats.

was preferable to the loss of core properties, and therefore that a working agreement with the Council should be sought. A meeting was held in early February 1948 between representatives of the Company (led by William Fanstone Dyer, Livery, 1911, Master, 1954, himself a surveyor) and of Deptford Council (led by Councillor W.J. Coombs, the Chairman of the Housing Committee) at which an agreement was thrashed out. It was agreed that the Council would compulsorily purchase sites on Erlanger Road, New Cross Road, Goodwood Road, and Batavia Road, and develop them with the Company's good will, but that it would abandon its plans with respect to Waller Road, and would not seek to develop other parts of the charity estate except with the trustees' full

18   Before and after: (i) Haberdashers' Place before demolition, 1951; (ii) Haberdashers' Place after rebuilding, 1955.

approval. The Company, for its part, agreed energetically to develop all other suitable sites on the estates as far as possible in line with the Council's plans. The Council, moreover, would give assistance to the Company in seeking to shift the Minister of Health's opposition to the Avignon Road development.[4] By 1949 the Company had secured the necessary consents to the development of flats on Waller Road and Avignon Road, the costs of £66,260 to be met from the Rebuilding Fund (which had been topped up with war damage value payments). However, the effect was to leave the Hatcham rebuilding fund with just £5,103.[5]

The low rates of return on residential developments – only about 3.33 per cent in the case of the Waller Road scheme – meant that the Company was reluctant to commit large amounts of capital, which in any case was in short supply, to projects of this kind. Commercial developments were preferred, but these had to be compatible with the local authority's zoning of areas as residential or industrial. The Aske Governors had been successful in securing building consents for expansion to the Bevenden House warehouse for use by an export company, and the charity had secured an 8.5 per cent return. In a report on the Hoxton estate in 1950, in which sale of the whole estate was considered, W.F. Dyer recommended retention and the concentration of resources on the development of the areas zoned for light industry, financing them by means of loans on the more modern buildings.[6]

There was some progress in the 1950s. The costs of rebuilding of Fanshawe House on the Hoxton estate, re-opened in November 1953, and occupied by Stock, Page, Stock, the Company's estate managers, were largely covered by means of the war damage payment.[7] Shoreditch Council's threat in 1951 to reschedule Styman Street as a residential rather than light industrial zone prompted the Company to press ahead with the development of factories on the site. Four factories were constructed over the next decade on the site of Styman Street and Chart Street: Truscott, Wakefield, Ebbisham, and Jenks Houses were named after Haberdasher Lord Mayors. Although the low level of the rebuilding fund meant that they had to be largely financed by loans (thus Truscott House, opened in 1956, cost £59,531 4s. 9d., and was paid for by a loan of £50,000 from the Commercial Union Assurance Company, with the balance from the rebuilding fund), the initial returns of around 8 per cent were impressive.[8] Meanwhile a major development scheme, financed by the proceeds from the sale of the unprofitable manor of Singleton in Kent, went ahead in Pitfield Street, where the foundation stone of Haberdashers' Place was laid on 1 July 1952. The combination of flats and shops in the development ensured a healthy return of 7.1 per cent on its completion in 1954.[9] On the Hatcham estate the surveyor put considerable work into repairs in the years after 1948, and the improvements were noticeable by 1952.[10] From 1956 there were major sales of residential properties on the periphery of the estate, which financed building works at the schools, and the development of low-rise flats in Arbuthnot and Jerningham Road (Wells House, Dyer House, and Eliott House opened in 1956, and Franklin House in 1957).[11] There was also an attempt to develop commercial properties within the local authority constraints on the Hatcham estate. Two warehouses were built on the Goodwood Road site, Bond House, opening in 1962, and Blundell House in 1964, offering returns of around 10 per cent. The total cost of Blundell House (including the value of the site at £41,000) was £316,023, and the rents received were £30,232 per annum. The warehouse needed to be financed by a consortium of the Company's minor charities (a decision opposed by some members of the Court), as the resources in the Jones fund were insufficient.[12]

The bulk of the charities' properties still remained residential, and offered a very low rate of return because of their rent-controlled status, and the high costs of repairs and management charges. The following figures from the Hatcham estate for 1962 and 1963 will give some idea of the scale of the problem:

Table 2.1: Rents on Hatcham estate, 1962-1963 (£)

	1962	1963
Gross rents	116,000	146,000
Rates	28,300	38,500
Repairs	23,100	36,500
Management	11,120	13,870
Rebuilding fund	6,960	8,760
Net rents	46,520	48,370

20 per cent of gross rents were allocated to repairs, 6 per cent to the rebuilding fund, and 9½ per cent to management charges. The effect of increases in the rates in a year in which gross rents increased by 25 per cent is plainly apparent; once the outgoings (calculated as a percentage of gross rents) were taken into account, net receipts had only grown by 4 per cent.[13]

The Company's capacity to engage in independent redevelopment schemes of its estates continued to face numerous obstacles. Although the Company tried to work in conjunction with the local authorities, the vagaries of local politics meant that, from the Company's point of view, there was a lack of focus and much inconsistency. In 1964 the Company's frustration over delays in the

L.C.C.'s submission of plans for new roads in the New Cross area resulted in a highly embarrassing article in the *Evening Standard*, in which the Haberdashers were quoted as condemning the plans as 'stupid and unfair'.[14] Moreover, as the financing of Blundell House suggests, the Haberdashers were seriously hampered by lack of capital resources, and they simply could not match the resources the local authorities could draw upon. One solution, tried in the early 1960s, was the formation of a Housing Society: the Company leased sites at current market rents to the Society which would then borrow 100 per cent of the cost of the works from the borough council or the L.C.C. for 60-70 years, and the rents of the residential units would be fixed to cover the costs of amortisation, rates, loans, management, and maintenance. In 1964 the Company attempted to head off a Compulsory Purchase Order on part of the Hoxton estate by Shoreditch Borough Council by coming up with its own development plan in association with the Haberdashers' Housing Society, but it had to concede that the Council's scheme was a better one. The Company could not afford to buy out the lessees' interests of three factories in the re-development area, and could therefore only undertake piecemeal redevelopment. In this situation the Council was unwilling to advance 100 per cent of the development costs, and the compulsory purchase went ahead.[15]

An alternative to re-development by the Company was the sale of the residential properties. The motives here were mixed. Property sales were a means of raising cash for development projects at the schools (the monies being replaced over a 30-year period), but alternatively the monies raised could be re-invested either in higher-yielding commercial properties or in securities. Until 1956 the Company's position had been that no freehold would be disposed of save by compulsory purchase order, but in that year the Hatcham Estates Advisory Committee, noting that political trends were unfavourable to the landlord, advised that properties becoming vacant should be sold rather than improved and re-let. Thus in the five years to the end of 1962, £627,560 was raised through property sales on the Hatcham estate.[16] Another large block was sold to Lewisham Borough Council in 1964 for £107,675, and receipts from sales averaged £86,776 per annum through the 1960s.[17] The sales helped finance about £1 million of essential building works at the schools in the years up to 1973, but some was retained for reinvestment.[18] Thus it was from the proceeds of the first tranche of sales in 1958 that the Company undertook the purchase for £230,000 of 90-91, Wood Street, an office block hard by Staining Lane, and thereafter named Hamersley House after a Haberdasher Lord Mayor of the 17th century. This represented an important shift from residential to higher yielding commercial investments for the Jones charity, a policy that was to be more consistently applied in the 1980s (Hamersley House offered an initial return of 6 per cent).[19]

The policy of piecemeal sales of properties continued through the 1960s, but increasingly voices were raised in favour of a policy of getting rid of all the residential properties. In April 1968, in view of continuing low returns and doubts about the security of landlords under a Labour administration,

19 Mr Harold Quitman (Master, 1979).

the Hatcham Estate Select Committee recommended that the Company should abandon the idea of redeveloping its residential properties, and seek instead to sell them to the local authority. But the radical proposal was not implemented, the Company adopting instead a wait-and-see approach, hoping for an initiative from the Council.[20] In 1973 they commissioned a report from the property consultants, Conrad Ritblat & Co., on the Hatcham and Hoxton estates. By this time the residential properties in the northern part of the Hatcham estate were only offering a 2.7 per cent return, and those in the southern part only 3 per cent; commercial properties returned a healthier 6.7 per cent, but this was still below expectations. On the Hoxton estate returns on residential properties were 3 per cent and those on commercial properties only 4.3 per cent. One problem was that the multi-storey units, like Blundell House and Bond House (Hatcham) and Bevenden House (Hoxton), were not in line with the current favour for single-storey units which could easily be partitioned. Conrad Ritblat recommended sales of blocks to developers, though retaining some of the better quality housing in the southern part of the Hatcham estate. Some Court members voiced anxieties about possible pressure being put on the tenants by the developers, and when another block was sold for £1.145 million in November 1974 the purchaser was Lewisham Borough Council.[21] The local authority's capacity to buy further blocks was constrained in the years ahead by a serious financial squeeze, as the economy nose-dived into recession in the wake of the oil price shock from November 1973 culminating in the sterling crisis of September 1976 and the stringent terms of the I.M.F. loan. Another block was sold to a 'breaker-upper'. But the policy of opportunistic sales was soon to be transformed by the more favourable climate provided by the Thatcher administration's coming to power in 1979.[22]

The election of a Conservative government coincided with the formation of the Company's Property Committee in 1979-80 during the Mastership of Harold Quitman (Livery, 1955). It was this which led to the implementation of a determined and consistent policy on selling the residential properties. Quitman advised the Court of Assistants that the manner in which property was managed needed modernisation. He recommended the establishment of a Property Committee which would be authorised by the corporate fund and each charity owning property of any kind to buy, sell, and otherwise deal with its property assets unconditionally. The Committee's remit thus extended not only to the residential properties that constituted the bulk of the Hatcham and Hoxton estates, but also the office buildings that were part of the corporate portfolio. It was an impressive committee. Deliberately kept small, it was much better suited to swift decisions on cumbrous agendas than the unwieldy Aske and Jones Committees which had combined discussion of estate matters with matters of educational policy. It was also staffed by appropriate experts. Harold Quitman was well equipped for the task. After six-and-a-half years' military service from 1939, he had become a director of the Aquis Property Company formed in 1905 to hold a number of high quality buildings throughout central London in the ownership of members of his maternal family. He worked to turn its fortunes around after severe war damage by means of investments in a series of residential and commercial developments. In due course he became Managing Director and Chairman, and eventually the company became quoted as Aquis Securities plc. Christopher Bostock (Livery, 1947, Master, 1983) had been apprenticed in 1937 to Gibson Harris (soon to become the Company's first auditor) and, after wartime service, had become a partner in his family's firm of chartered accountants, Annan Dexter, in 1952, but later moved into management consultancy, and then professional management. The Committee was undoubtedly dominated by Quitman whose working career had given him a taste for an entrepreneurial approach to property and a healthy scepticism about professional advisers! However, he gathered a team of advisers he could trust. One of the first actions of the Property Committee was to divide the professional management by using firms of surveyors who specialised in the various spheres. For City properties the firm of Debenham Tewson and Chinnocks (represented by Keith Way) was used; for shops and industrial investment advice was taken from Conrad Ritblat & Co. (represented by Bob Bowden), and for residential properties Stock, Page, Stock (represented by Christopher Maunder-Taylor). It was an outstanding and highly effective team. It was also an extremely hard-working committee. Initially it met eight times

20   Mr Christopher Bostock (Master, 1983).

a year, and worked from 11.00 am until a lunch break in the Hall, and then again afterwards until 4.00 pm or sometimes even later.[23]

The policy that Quitman now advocated was that, rather than selling off blocks of property at discounted prices, the Company should undertake the breaking up of the estate itself. The senior partner of the Company's property managers, Stock, Page, Stock, expressed reservations, but Christopher Maunder-Taylor, a junior partner in the firm, agreed to undertake the job, and to do it in such a way as not to bring damage to the reputation of the Company. There is no doubt that there were from time to time elements of a culture clash between Quitman's hard-headed approach to the maximisation of income from the investments and the more paternalist values of other members of the Court. Quitman recalled that he had to fight hard against the reservations of some of his colleagues, but that the argument with which he prevailed was the Company's obligations as charitable trustees to maximise the income of its charities. As Quitman put it to his committee in 1984, 'the position was clear, viz. That the properties must in all cases be sold to the highest bidder since any other policy would be condemned by the Charity Commission'.[24] The policy encountered some local opposition which sensitised its critics on the Court. In 1983 a Haberdashers' Tenants Association alleged harassment

21   Boddington and Boulter Charity property at 289/294 Bishopsgate Street.

but a visit from the then Deputy Clerk (Michael Barrow) and Maunder-Taylor on 22 June found no evidence of action that might bring the Company into disrepute, and several tenants expressed their confidence in the integrity of the Estate Manager.[25]

The break up took 13 years, but proceeded at its swiftest in the early years. Between March 1980 and March 1991 the Jones charity had received a total of £14,735,243 from sales at Hatcham and Monmouth, and the Aske charity £2,395,529 from sales at Hoxton.[26] In 1991 the Company considered selling the rump to a developer. In the face of criticism from some members of the Court, Quitman pressed for complete disengagement from the estate, 'the present policy had been pursued for too long now to be reversed, for the point was being reached where only a rump would be left, on any view fit only for disposal'.[27] In the event the tenders for the rump were below the stock value, so the policy of piecemeal sales continued for another two years until August 1993, when the rump was sold to Frogmore Developments Ltd for £3.835 million.[28] By the time the last properties were disposed of, total receipts had been over £20 million.[29] Whatever the occasional frictions the policy had produced, the Court expressed its appreciation of the extraordinary labours of Quitman and his committee. In 1983 they awarded him a methusalah of Pol Roger champagne, and in 1994, on his retirement from the chairmanship of the committee, they presented him with a Chippendale silver salver engraved with the Company's arms.[30]

Although the bulk of the Property Committee's business was concerned with the sales on the Hoxton and Hatcham estates, there were opportunities elsewhere. The Boddington and Boulter charity owned a multi-storey industrial building dating from the late 19th century at 284/294 Bishopsgate. In 1978 the charity was credited with assets of £60,000 (the property was leased at £800 per annum with 28 years of the lease still to run), but an offer of £100,000 had already been received for it, as it provided a significant part of the Bishopsgate frontage for what later became the redevelopment of Spitalfields Market. As a result of negotiations with the developers the price increased to the point where the property was eventually sold for £3 million in 1986. It was this 'windfall' which was a major factor behind the establishment of the Haberdashers' Charities Investment Property Pool, and a more ambitious approach to charitable support.[31]

The proceeds of the sales were invested in a ratio of roughly 50:50 between realty and personalty. Suitable investments in commercial properties with a return of 6 per cent were identified by Conrad Ritblat & Co.[32] In 1987 it was decided to pool the property resources of the various charities, allowing for greater flexibility in acquisitions, each charity drawing on income in proportion to its investment. Unfortunately, the pool was established shortly before a decline in property values set in. Equities out-performed property through the early '90s, and the wisdom of a high exposure to property was increasingly questioned, especially in the light of other charities and pension funds having limited their property exposure to 5-10 per cent.[33] In 1997 (shortly after the substantial realisation from the sale of Hamersley House in 1996) it was decided to dispose gradually of all properties in the Charities Investment Pool, and to re-invest in property unit trusts, while reducing the property exposure of the Jones charity from 25 per cent to 15 per cent. The bulk of the property pool was sold for £9.2 million in October 1997, leaving only Truscott House in Hoxton and retail property in Maidstone in the pool.[34]

The other major policy shift of the early 1980s was a change in the means by which the schools had financed capital projects. As we have seen, some of the major school projects of the 1960s and 1970s were financed by cash raised on the sale of properties. At Monmouth these projects included an assembly hall, two swimming pools, a large gymnasium, a residential block, and a series of new teaching spaces. When the Aske Girls' School moved to Elstree, part of the finance came from the sale of flats on the Hoxton estate.[35] In 1980 a sub-committee chaired by Christopher Bostock, a self-styled life-long warrior against inflation, proposed new methods for financing capital projects designed to avoid the diminution of the funds. By the terms of the 'Bostock Rules' as they became known, interest-free loans could be made to the schools for capital projects repayable over a maximum period of 15 years, the repayments being indexed to the level of inflation. In the past the schools had been allowed to replace monies taken for capital projects in equal annual instalments over a 30-year period. Given the ravages of inflation, the replacement covered less and less of the original capital, so that the capital fund was eroded. The Bostock rules were designed to ensure that the real value of the advances from capital was refunded. They proved initially controversial. Fraser Bird (Livery, 1936, Master, 1972) did not want the principle followed slavishly to the point where the continued existence of the schools would be imperilled; Pat Powell (Livery, 1932, Master, 1969), as Chairman of Governors of the Monmouth

Schools, thought the new rules too dogmatic, and expressed anxiety about the possible impact on the level of the school fees as the Governors struggled to repay their loans. It was an emotive discussion over which the demons of out-of-control inflation loomed. Peter Jenks (Livery, 1962) spoke frankly of the possibility of schools collapsing, explaining that 'if schools were ailing to a degree which made it plain that they could not survive much longer, there must come a point at which the trustees would be bound to say enough was enough and would have to devote themselves entirely to the preservation of what remained of the funds without which the Company would have little purpose'. To Powell's objections, Quitman retorted that the rules were designed to meet the worst case scenario of continuing high inflation, but that if the Conservative government's counter-inflation strategy failed, 'the country would become a "banana republic" and the outlook for private education would be bleak, as would the prospects for any kind of enterprise'. After some concessions to meet the problems of the Monmouth Governors who had embarked on a new science block before knowing about the new rules, the Bostock Rules were adopted.[36]

The transforming effect of the 'Quitman/Bostock years' on the major charities is plainly apparent from the data in Table 2.2.

Table 2.2: Aske and Jones Charities, essential figures in 1999 prices (£000s)

HABERDASHERS' ASKE'S CHARITY

	1958	1961	1970	1980	1990	1995
Investment assets						
Property	3669	3866	1843	1227	5299	2762
Securities	645	595	939	750	4194	7068
Bostock loans					1489	1844
Distributable income	219	446	446	252	425	518

WILLIAM JONES'S SCHOOLS FOUNDATION

	1958	1961	1970	1980	1990	1995
Investment assets						
Property	3097	3045	1925	2682	22564	11817
Securities	2747	5133	4954	4872	18718	29936
Bostock loans					2385	2688
Distributable income	532	937	1128	1240	2151	2132

Comparing financial trends over time is rendered difficult by the effects of inflation. The retail price index rose from 158 in 1960 (on a base of 100 in 1947) to 2091 in 1999. To produce more meaningful data the figures in the tables have been converted to 1999 prices: on that basis the income of the Jones charity in 1958 was £532,000 and in 1995 £2.132 million, a four-fold increase in real terms. Closer examination reveals significant shifts in the period 1960-90. There was only very modest growth in the twenty years after 1960, as the charity sold property to fund capital projects. The 1980s saw a remarkable turn-around. Over the course of the decade the investment asets were boosted by the inclusion of the receipts from sales on the Hatcham estate which amounted to £13.5 million, to which should be added £1.5 million from sales in Monmouth, and a 'profit' of £9.7 million when Hamersley House was transferred to the Charitable Property Pool at market value. Income nearly doubled from £1.24 million in 1980 to £2.151 million in 1980.[37]

The capital of the Aske charity was adversely affected by the cost of the moves to Elstree, as the following data makes clear:

Table 2.3: Cost of school building at Elstree

	Actual prices	1999 equivalent prices
Boys' school (1961-2)		
Cost of site and building works	£488,000	£5,761,000
Sale proceeds of Hampstead School	£255,000	£3,006,000
Net cost	£233,000	£2,755,000
Girls' school (1973-4)		
Cost of site and works	£1,514,000	£6,600,000
Sale proceeds of Acton School	£706,000	£3,312,000
Net cost	£808,000	£3,388,000

The short-fall in the financing of the boys' school was covered largely by a loan from the charity, but in the case of the girls' school some higher yielding investment properties, including flats and commercial properties (Aske House and Jenks House), on the Hoxton estate were sold. The result was that the available income stagnated in real terms in the 1960s and fell markedly in the 1980s. The more effective management of the 1980s is clear in the recovery of income levels, but the Aske charity has overall performed less well than Jones because of the sales to finance capital projects at the schools. (Table 2.2).[38]

Thus far we have detailed the fortunes of the finances underpinning the Company's charities. It is now time to turn to the corporate income. Throughout the period under review the financial health of the Company has depended upon a small number of properties. In 1949-50, for example, the corporate accounts reveal that rents contributed £14,850 (78 per cent) to a total income of £18,960; dividends on investments amounted to £2,162 (11.4 per cent), and admission fees and quarterage to £1,670 (8.8 per cent). In 2000-1 property continued to provide the bulk of income, contributing £806,954 (78 per cent) as compared with £209,426 (20 per cent) in dividends and interest, and an exiguous £5,435 (0.5 per cent) in membership income. The relative predominance of property income conceals considerable change within the portfolio, and in its revenue-earning capacity. In 1950 the bulk of revenue came from two properties, 37 and 38 Lombard Street, leased respectively to the

Netherlands Bank of South Africa and The United Dominions Property Trust Ltd for the sums of £5,000 per annum and £7,000 per annum respectively. There were a handful of other freeholds in the city and wider metropolitan area: 36-42 New Inn Yard, Shoreditch (£300 per annum), Central House, Finsbury (£500 per annum), Fulwood House, Holborn (£500 per annum), 119, Queen Victoria Street (£120 per annum), Popesgrove Mansions, Heath Road, Twickenham (£325 per annum), and some houses in Hillcroft Crescent, Ealing (£96 18s. per annum). There were two farms Walton Hall at High Ercall in Shropshire and Cold Kirby located between Helmsley and Thirsk in Yorkshire on yearly tenancies yielding an average of £564 per annum and £1,306 per annum respectively in the early 1950s. Cold Kirby had been purchased in 1950 as an investment of corporate funds pending the redevelopment of the Hall site. Because of the effects of war damage, leases had been disclaimed on a number of properties the bulk of them in the vicinity of the Staining Lane Hall: the combined loss in rental income on the corporate account as compared with the pre-war levels was £3,945 per annum. In 2000-1 the bulk of the property income came from the site of the old Hall and Garrard House, together recently rebuilt as 31, Gresham Street, although other income would be due to come on stream from the Weddel House frontage to the new Hall and the adjoining office block in Hosier Lane. The other freeholds, apart from Fulwood House, had been sold over the course of the previous fifty years.[39] Those bald facts conceal a rather more complex story.

The Company withdrew from its agricultural properties in the 1950s. The Cold Kirby farm was only showing a return of 1.83 per cent, and capital improvements were necessary to bring it into line with the requirements of the County Milk Production Officer. The farm was sold in 1955 for £31,000 (£4,000 less than the original asking price), providing the shortfall between receipts from the War Damage Commission (£113,750) and the cost of constructing the new Hall in Staining Lane (£139,485). Walton Hall was sold in 1958 for £37,000 (£33,980 net).[40] The charities had also disinvested from agricultural properties in this decade with the sale of Jones' Singleton manor in Kent in 1951 and the Knighton estate in Shropshire belonging to the Adams Charity in 1956.[41] There were occasional explorations into the possibility of agricultural investments, but the position was summed up by the Court of Assistants bluntly in 1972: 'it is now clear that it [agricultural land] is no longer a worthwhile investment'.[42]

A more important change with long-term implications was the opening in 1956 of the office block on the Company's freehold property surrounding the new post-war Hall. Financial backing for Garrard House, as the building was called, had been provided by the Legal and General Assurance Society, to whom it was leased for 99 years at a rent of £6,000 per annum. Even as this agreement was being entered into some Court members recognised the likelihood that the value of the rent would be eroded by inflation: in 1955, on the eve of its opening, a proposal that the rent be commuted was seriously considered on the grounds of the possible long-term erosion of income.[43] In the event, inflation did seriously undermine the growth potential of the corporate

22   Garrard House office development, incorporating first post-war Hall,
on opening in 1956.

income. The scale of the loss of income is indicated by the fact that Legal and
General had granted an under-lease to the Church Commissioners for £35,000
per annum. Harold Quitman, during his term as Second Warden, meeting the
Permanent Secretary to the Church Commissioners socially, and subsequently
with Legal and General's man dealing with Garrard House, suggested that as
the leases concerned had diminished in length by some years, there might be
advantage in a renegotiation of terms. Although it took some time to bring
Legal and General round to this view (they had in the meantime bought
out the Church Commissioners' interest becoming head lessee), by 1982 the
Company got its way, negotiating more favourable terms: the property was
now leased for 125 years, with the Company receiving 11 per cent rising over
three years to 14 per cent of rents received by Legal and General, with a
guaranteed minimum income of £144,000, this minimum being subject to rent
review every 15 years to 10 per cent of rental value. An immediate premium
of £250,000 was paid to assist the Company in solving its accommodation
problems. An option was also taken on the ground floor of Garrard House,
to enable the Hall accommodation to be expanded as and when that floor
was vacated by the occupying tenant. The negotiations had been handled
by Quitman's Property Committee and Debenham Tewson & Chinnocks, the
surveyors, and they had pressed as tough a bargain as they could, driving
up the proportion of rents receivable and insisting upon the premium. The
renegotiated lease transformed the Company's corporate financial position for
the remainder of the 1980s.[44]

The renegotiation of the Garrard House lease was typical of the more
entrepreneurial attitude towards its properties that the Company developed
around this time. It had really missed out on the first boom in the provision

of city office accommodation in the 1950s, but it was determined not to repeat the error in the second boom. The lessees of Fulwood Place in High Holborn in 1972 offered to buy the freehold but Harold Quitman and Gordon Bourne (Livery, 1963, Master, 1984: he joined the Property Committee in 1985) argued against a sale whatever the short-term boost to corporate income, because they felt that the property would appreciate substantially in value in the succeeding years. Interestingly the offer level rose from £50,000 to £90,000 but still the Company held out, arguing that it wanted to participate in a redevelopment scheme to benefit from the enhanced value of the property.[45] In 1976 Quitman received permission from the Master to negotiate the future of this property. Working with Jones Lang Wootton as surveyors, the Company arranged a bank loan of £100,000 which was used to buy out the occupying tenants' leases. With vacant possession Jones Lang Wootton obtained a developer partner (Property Growth Assurance) prepared to renovate the now vacant building, meeting the whole cost, and who would pay a premium for a lease sufficient to pay off the bank loan, and pass 25 per cent of the annual rents to the Company. With a pre-let to Denton's (solicitors) there was the prospect of a rent of £54,000 per annum with reviews at five-year intervals. But within days of the signature of the contract, Property Growth withdrew, expressing lack of confidence in the government's fiscal policies (it was the height of the IMF crisis of the Callaghan administration). Quitman, who recalls receiving a large whisky from the then Master, David Sime (Livery, 1950, Master, 1976 and 1989) as the news broke, felt a degree of personal responsibility for this near-disaster, but was vindicated by the Court. There were some nail-biting months ahead with the Company confronted by an empty building, with no income, and saddled with a large loan. Offers to buy the freehold were resisted, and in the event after a year Haslemere Estates took on the leasehold for 125 years, agreeing on a premium of £200,000, and 10 per cent of the rack rents. It was a good outcome for the enhanced value of the property was considerably in excess of the £90,000 that had been offered for the freehold a few years earlier.[46]

Likewise, with the still more valuable 37/38 Lombard Street properties, the lost opportunities of the 1960s were succeeded by a more aggressively commercial attitude. The Company, to the frustration of some of the Assistants (led by W.F. Dyer who suspected that a more proactive stance might have achieved better results), had lost the chance to participate in a development scheme involving neighbouring properties owned by the Fishmongers' Company in 1964 and 1969, because of the unfavourable terms on which the lessees were prepared to surrender.[47] Nevertheless, when the lease of 38, Lombard Street was assigned to Northern Trust Company of Chicago in 1969, the Haberdashers agreed to contribute £130,000 to the cost of improvements in the property subject to a 9.5 per cent return with a further rent review in 1975.[48] At that review the rent was raised to £165,435 per annum, achieving a net increase to corporate income of £65,000 per annum.[49] A chance to maximise the income flow for the adjacent 37, Lombard Street came in 1983, the redevelopment being undertaken by Guinness Peat Property Services Ltd under a development

23 31 Gresham Street, the new headquarters of
Schroders International, opened in 1998.

agreement with the Company. The property was to be leased for 125 years
with the Haberdashers receiving 47.5 per cent of the rents passing. Willingness
to participate in redevelopment schemes thus considerably enhanced the value
of the corporate property portfolio.[50]

However, the risks of the Company's high level of exposure to property and
its dependence on a small number of city freeholds became apparent in the
ending of the city property boom as the 1980s turned into the 1990s. Plans
to redevelop Garrard House in association with Legal and General had to be
shelved, and when the sub-leases fell in in 1990 it emerged that the building
would only be 40 per cent occupied, meaning that the income fell to the
minimum level of £144,000 and, although with some aggressive marketing of
the voids there was some recovery by the mid-1990s (rent received in 1994-5
was £181,800), this was below the late 1980s levels.[51] The growth in value
of the other city properties was halted, a point graphically illustrated by the
fact that whereas 38 Lombard Street was valued at £6.9 million in 1989,
three years later it was only £4 million.[52] It was in these circumstances that
the Company began to consider divesting itself of some of the key freeholds
to reduce exposure to property, and establish the ratio between property and
personalty in tune with current trends. It was a policy which left some members
of the Court profoundly uneasy, both because of a sentimental attachment
to sites which had been in the Company's possession since the 17th century,
and because they could not understand the logic of selling, as it were, 'at the

bottom of the market'. It was decided nonetheless in 1992, in the face of what Christopher Bostock as Chairman of the Finance Committee called 'inexorable logic', to put 37/38 Lombard Street on the market; their sale would leave the Company with Fulwood House and Garrard House, representing 25 per cent of corporate assets, which was felt to be a healthier position. Because of their listed building status, redevelopment of the Lombard Street properties was impossible, and some pretty derisory offers (including one of just £2 million for no. 38) were received from bargain hunters, so the Haberdashers had to sit tight until the summer of 1994. No. 38 was sold for £3.53 million net (inclusive of dilapidations) on 19 August 1994, but it was decided to retain No. 37 for the time being because the return on any stock market investment of the anticipated proceeds of a sale would be below the current rent receipts of £189,000 pa.[53] No. 37 was eventually sold in 2000 for £2.07 million net, the receipts helping to fund the commercial development of Hosier Lane as part of the West Smithfield project.[54]

The effect of these sales was to leave Garrard House as the key to corporate success. Fulwood House was retained, but it is a very modest property. By 1995 the Garrard House block was long past its sell-by date, and the Haberdashers had long realised that only a redeveloped office block on that site would offer the possibility of real income growth. The story of the Company's several false starts in negotiations with Legal and General for a redevelopment will be told in the final chapter. But here it needs to be stressed that a move of the Hall away from the Staining Lane site and the construction of a new office block on the Garrard House and old Hall site would result in a major boost to corporate resources. In 1996 therefore the Company reached terms with Legal and General, by which it would receive a premium of £9 million and 9.5 per cent of the rents passing subject to a guaranteed minimum of £300,000 per annum, which is subject to upward only review every 17 years. The Company's income of 9.5 per cent of rents passing is effectively subject to review every five years because it is derived from rents paid by Schroders Investment Management as sub-tenants, the rent under their occupation lease being subject to rent review every five years.[55] When the block was opened in 1998 the rents received were £584,159.94 per annum (more than three times that received from the old building in its last years).[56] Although the construction of the new Hall in West Smithfield in 2002 proved much more expensive than had been optimistically anticipated in 1995, the decision to undertake the development of the commercial properties adjoining in Hosier Lane promises an additional income stream. Although the Company faces a number of lean years (one indication of which is the revival in 2003 of quarterage payments from Liverymen), an aggressive approach to the marketing of the new Hall and the successful marketing of the Hosier Lane properties should combine to restore the finances to an even keel by 2005-6.[57] But that outcome depends on a buoyant economy and continuing demand for property within the City, because, in spite of the achievement of a better balance between realty and personalty in the early 1990s, the Company's corporate assets remain vulnerable to swings in City property values.

24   Company property at 38, Lombard Street,
the building in the centre.

Nevertheless, the performance of the corporate funds over the long term should leave the Company satisfied. The dramatic turn-around in performance is clear, and demonstrates the effects of the more commercial approach taken to the corporate property.[58] Whether we look at income levels or the rate of growth of corporate income earning assets, the change in the Company's fortunes in the 1980s is apparent. In the 1950s and 1960s there was only modest growth in income earning assets, but income levels grew markedly in the 1950s, more slowly in the 1960s. In the 1970s increases in the valuation of the properties consequent upon enhanced rent levels for Fulwood House and Lombard Street were offset by the fall in stock exchange investments consequent on the oil price shock of 1973-4, but the value of the income earning funds was still 17 per cent higher in real terms in 1980 than ten years previously. Then the Company entered its boom period of spectacular growth in the 1980s with assets 41 per cent higher in real terms in 1990 than 1980 and income levels 73 per cent higher in real terms. That growth reflects the revisions in rent levels from Garrard House and further favourable reviews on the Lombard Street properties. If income levels have fallen in the 1990s that has been a reflection of the temporary switch in investments in the mid-1990s to securities and a policy of capital growth. Overall, income-earning assets still grew by 5.3 per cent in real terms over the decade.[59]

The 1990s were in many respects a period of consolidation. Although the decade began with the corporate account in an unhealthy position because of the sluggish economy and low demand for property, the foundations had been laid to ensure a prompt recovery. A number of important measures were also taken in order to reduce the Company's exposure to tax. Of these the most important was the establishment in 1995 and 1996 of subsidiary companies. In 1995 the Company identified that significant elements of the Hall's administrative expenses were allowable as the expenses of the holding company, the Haberdashers' Management Company (H.M.C.), and subject to corporation tax relief. In the following year the Haberdashers' Management Company (Garrard House) was set up so that the Company and the H.M.C. would not be affected by the V.A.T. potentially chargeable on the rents received from Garrard House. The overall effect of these measures was to save £66,000 in taxation in the year ending March 1997, albeit with some modest increases in professional fees.[60] By 1998 the prospect of constructing the new Hall meant that it would be beneficial for the Company to register for V.A.T., which was implemented from 1 April that year: this would enable the Company to reclaim a proportion of the V.A.T. payable on the building of the new Hall. Registration for V.A.T. brought about the rearrangement of the subsidiary companies on a more logical basis as a fair amount of juggling had been necessary to keep their resources below the V.A.T. threshold. The Haberdashers' Management Company was renamed as the Haberdashers' Investment Company (H.I.C.) while the Haberdashers' Management Company (Garrard House) was renamed as the Haberdashers' Operating Company (H.O.C.). This has enabled the Worshipful Company to concentrate on its core activities while the H.I.C. and H.O.C. subsidiaries look after stock market investments and investment property respectively.[61]

The story of the Company's financial transformations is essential to the rest of this book, as, without the successful management of its charitable resources, the path of the schools' development would have been very different, and improvements in corporate income have been essential to the quality of the Company's social life. We shall return to finances again at several points in the chapters which follow: building projects at the schools, the move of the Aske schools to Elstree, the continuing heavy subsidy to fees at Monmouth schools would have been impossible without effective financial management by the Company and the respective Governors. The diversification of charitable activity entailed has also depended on the more effective management of the charitable investments. Likewise, the diversification of the Company's social programme, its outreach to more elements of the Haberdasher community, and the construction of a new home in West Smithfield depended on the foundations laid by those who managed its finances in the last 25 years of the 20th century.

Chapter Three

The Organisation of the Company

At the end of the war in 1945, the Haberdashers were essentially operating under a committee structure which had been established in the 19th century. The most important standing committees, Finance, Estates, and Charities, had been set up in the reorganisation of 1826; in 1877 the Company added the Endowed Schools Committee and the Officers' and Clerk's Committee.[1] Additional committees might be constituted to deal with particular problems: thus a Planning Committee was established in 1947 to deal with issues pertaining to the reconstruction of the Hall. An ad hoc committee was set up to make the arrangements for the 500th anniversary of the charter in 1948.[2] There is no doubting that this structure placed considerable demands on Assistants, and particularly on the Master and Wardens who were ex officio members of most of them: in 1948 there were 12 meetings of the Court of Assistants, 15 meetings of the Estates Committee, eight of the Finance Committee, six of the Charities Committee, and five of the Endowed Schools Committee.[3]

A desire to reduce the burden on Assistants has lain behind a number of reforms, though not all of them can be counted a success. In 1958 the Company abolished the Endowed Schools Committee, replacing it with two advisory committees for the Jones and Aske charities, which dealt with matters of educational policy, reporting to the Finance and Estates Committees, but the new committees were to consume their masters, for in 1961 by a sweeping reform they absorbed the business of the Estates and Finance Committees. The recommendation for this, which was the product of a committee consisting of Lord Moynihan (Livery, 1930, Master, 1963), Robin Brook (Livery, 1932, Master, 1965), Bobby Shaw (Livery, 1931, Master, 1964), and Fraser Bird, was controversial, encountering opposition from W.F. Dyer and Bernard Elliott (Livery, 1911, Master, 1956) on the Court, but it was approved by 17 to 8 votes. The result was to create two 'super committees', the Jones Charity and the Aske Charity Committees, dealing with educational matters and the complex management of the charity properties and the financing of school building projects. As there were in effect only four committees (these two plus the Minor Charities, and Wine Committees) the number of meetings was reduced.[4] The new committees had unwieldy agendas, while the lack of a Finance Committee meant that much of the responsibility for strategic thinking about financial matters rested by default with the Court of Wardens where there was less continuity and not necessarily the right spread of expertise. Robin Brook may have come to regret his involvement in the 1961 reform, for he was the architect and Chairman of the Finance Committee which was established in 1968, soon reconstituted in 1969 as the Finance and Estates Committee.[5]

25   Court of Assistants, 19 November 1945 at Vintners' Hall on the admission of Field Marshal
Sir Harold Alexander to freedom and Livery.

Nevertheless some Court members were suspicious of the power of the new
committee, and in 1972 Fraser Bird, then First Warden, complained that it had
taken decisive action on some estate questions (in particular the exchange of
the Wellington Road playing fields at Newport) without referring matters to the
appropriate standing committee. Brook was stung by the criticism asserting that
his committee had taken no action save on matters referred to it by standing
committees or the Court of Assistants: in the case of the playing fields he
asserted that the decision of substance had been taken elsewhere, and his
committee had merely implemented it. The committee survived this onslaught,
but it is striking that the Jones and Aske Committees continued to handle the
day-to-day management of the estates.[6] It was not until the establishment of
the Property Committee in 1980 that the Company acquired the mechanism
to take a more strategic view of its corporate and charity properties.[7] In 1982,
at the instigation of Dick Liddiard (Livery, 1939, Master, 1977), the committee
structure was further rationalised as the Aske and Monmouth committees,
now relieved of the burden of property management, were amalgamated into

a single Schools Committee.[8] There remained the problem of the relationship of the various financial committees to each other, especially as the situation was complicated by the establishment of the Investment Policy Committee also in 1982. It was decided in 1986 that this later committee should become the Finance Committee, which in turn would have oversight of the Property (Investment) Committee and the Securities (Investment) Committee. The Finance Committee would take the strategic decisions, particularly about the balance between realty and personalty, while the two subordinate committees would implement them. It is intriguing to note that the resultant core structure (dominated by committees for Finance, Schools, and Charities) was not unlike that operating immediately after the Second World War![9]

Overhaul of the structure and composition of committees was undertaken in both 1989 and in action subsequent to the 1999 corporate review. Both schemes had similar objectives: in 1989 to make more cost effective use of the time of Court members, ensuring that Assistants became familiar with the business of the Court at an early stage, and to ensure continuity in decision making. The 1999 review had among its objectives a desire to 'streamline the governance of the Company in recognition of increasing pressure on busy members to enable them to concentrate more on strategic issues', and to 'delegate routine decision making and management of Company affairs where appropriate'. In 1989 it was recognised that it was unreasonable to expect all Assistants below the chair to serve on a committee every year, and it was agreed that new Assistants should serve for two years on the Schools Committee and two years on the Charities Committee; thereafter they might serve again on these committees or be appointed to a school Governorship.[10] In 1999 (reiterating a concern of the 1989 review) it was recognised that the 'induction process' for new Assistants needed to be improved with the provision of briefing packs and encouragement to act as observers ('in attendance') at other committees. The 1999 review gave more thought to the question of continuity in decision making and the relationship between committees. Rather than having the Master chair the Charities and Education Committees, the review recommended that the Chairman be elected for a three-year term to ensure greater continuity. Efforts have been made to improve communication between the Company's schools and the Education Committee by requiring that the Chairmen of Governors of the schools attend one of the meetings of the Education Committee each year, and by ensuring that its members are people with recent experience as school Governors. The Education and Charities Committees have been better integrated with the Finance Committee by the requirement that their Chairmen be members of the Finance Committee. A simple but perhaps long overdue reform was the decision that minutes should not be gone through page by page in the Court of Assistants, but that key issues only should be identified for proper debate.[11]

It should be stressed, however, that the Court of Assistants retains a sensitivity over its powers of review over committee decisions and has a proper role in policy formulation. In 1950 members of the Court asserted that the selection

committee established to find a new Clerk had exceeded its powers, by making
a recommendation without giving the opportunity for a full interview by the
Court. That sensitivities ran high is suggested by the response to a proposal
from the Finance Committee in the same year to cut Court gifts to the level of
those for attendance at committees. Several Assistants opposed the measure on
the grounds that it implied a reduction in the Court's powers.[12] In 1964 some
Assistants felt that they were being kept in the dark about the negotiations
over the possible redevelopment of the Lombard Street properties.[13] There has
likewise been resistance to the suggestion of reducing the number of Court
meetings. In 1969 the number of Court meetings was reduced from 11 to six
on a temporary basis in the interests of economy, but members made it clear
that they wanted to revert to the normal schedule as soon as possible.[14] The
1999 corporate review recommended a reduction in the number of meetings
of the Court from 11 to eight, but in the event only the April Court meeting
has been dropped, leaving the Court with ten meetings per annum, a very
modest change.[15]

The Company has adapted to the changing management culture of the City
where the bulk of its members work. The 1980s saw the beginnings of the
concern for strategic planning. The first Corporate Review was undertaken
under Christopher Bostock's Mastership in 1983-4 and concerned itself with
the membership and ways in which the additional monies arising from the
renegotiated Garrard House lease could be used to best advantage.[16] At the same
time the Schools were encouraged to come up with 'five year plans', particularly
with a view to planning their building programmes better, and relating their
financing to endowment and school income.[17] There was a greater willingness to
use consultants, rather controversially in 1972 over the implications of possible
loss of direct grant status for Monmouth, but increasingly over a wider range
of activities, including the use of information technology in 1992-3.[18] Head
hunters were rejected in the quest for a Clerk in 1982 on the grounds of the
esoteric nature of the Clerk's duties which would be difficult to communicate
to the consultants. However, when Michael Barrow's successor was sought in
1994-5, recruitment advisers were employed to produce a short-list of six from
340 applicants: interestingly enough the Company selected another ex-naval
Clerk![19]

There has been some move in the direction of greater informality in meetings
again in line with broader changes in the City culture. In the mid-1960s it
was still customary for the Master and Wardens and Clerk to attend meetings
of the Court of Assistants in morning dress and gown, while Assistants wore
lounge suits with white shirts and stiff collars. The wearing of morning dress
was abandoned (as Commander Miller wryly pointed out, the gowns had
in any case concealed what lay beneath!), and a variety of shirts began to
proliferate. In 1979, in an attempt to balance the demands of dignity of the
Court with the preferences of individuals, it was recommended that white
shirts with attached white collars should be worn, 'or as a matter of individual
preference, a modestly coloured or striped shirt with stiff white collar': it was

26 Commander Bill Miller, Clerk (1966-83).

particularly important that this level of sartorial decorum was maintained on occasions when the Court was entertaining outside visitors, or appearing in public.[20]

Modernisation and professionalisation have been consistent goals pursued by the Company; they have perhaps at times vied with the values of 'fraternity', which is what makes the Livery Companies very different from other forms of charitable organisation. The cycle of Company meetings is enjoyed as much for the opportunities of sociability they afford as for the involvement of members in decision making. Meetings customarily take place in the late mornings and are followed by lunches. The author, brought up in the restrained traditions of Oxbridge colleges, was surprised at the opportunity to drink port at lunch time, when embarking on his original history in the mid-1980s; he has noted that Haberdasher luncheons of the new millennium are now characterised by a much higher degree of abstention. Gone also are the days recalled by senior members of the Court when the bridge tables (and more port!) came out after Court lunches.[21] But conviviality remains a key element in participation, and helps explain why Haberdashers are willing to give up so much of their time to the Company's business. Gone are the incentives of Court and committee attendance fees abolished in 1969,[22] but commensality remains central to corporate identity, not least for the opportunity for informal discussion of Company business and the nurturing of contacts within the Company's educational, charitable, and military spheres. Thus periodic proposals to switch the time of meetings to the late afternoon (5 pm) have not met with much support. There was an experiment in 1969 but it was dropped the following year; when the Company returned to the proposal in 1983 it was kicked into touch with the remark that it was necessary for members to get to know one another, and it was easier to do that 'over lunch than over a quick drink' after a meeting.[23] The corporate review of 1999 recommended that as far as committees were concerned, chairmen should have discretion to determine an appropriate time in consultation with members; as for the Court it was recommended that the existing single evening meeting in May should be supplemented by another in September, a move which was not universally supported by the older members and those living some way from London.[24]

The selection of Assistants is one of the most critical decisions the Company takes, because in selecting an Assistant the Company is in effect declaring that an individual has the qualities eventually to become Master. The mechanism by which Assistants are selected has been reformed to ensure that patronage and kinship ties play less of a part. As we shall see in the next chapter, a more rigorous attitude towards the selection of the Livery has come to prevail, as members with the right connections are no longer made free and clothed with the Livery on the same day. The same tendency towards professionalisation is apparent in the selection of Assistants. It is revealing that the Standing Orders Committee reported in 1952 that the Junior Wardens should no longer be selected by seniority only: rather one should be according to seniority and the other according to expertise. It was further suggested that there should be more detailed examination of the qualifications for high office, but that there should be no hard and fast rule about whether those nominated for the Junior Wardenships should be employers or employees.[25] In 1958 it was decided that each year the Master and Wardens accompanied by two Past Masters and an Assistant would entertain those Liverymen eligible by seniority, and those thought suitable for office would be invited on a school deputation. The Master and Wardens would make recommendations to the Court on the basis of the impressions formed at these events.[26] In 1961 the practice of electing the Junior Warden direct from the Livery was abandoned, and the office came to be filled by Assistants of some three to four years' standing.[27] By 1985 it was customary to ensure that there were at least two candidates for each vacancy on the Court, and selection was by interview only, to ensure competitive standards of entry.[28] Nevertheless from time to time Assistants have found the burden of their commitment to the Company incompatible with the demands of professional life, and others have realised that they are not up to the pressures of high office (in particular, skill in chairing committees and public speaking), and they have accepted the status of Honorary Assistant with a continued right to sit on the Court but without voting rights. In the wake of the corporate review of 1999, the Company established a new standing committee, the Membership and Appointments Committee, consisting of the

Master, First and Second Wardens, and three Past Masters under the age of 70. Its responsibilities extend not only to the identification of Liverymen suitable for election as Assistants, but also to the assessment of the suitability of Assistants for high office, and ensuring that the preferences of Assistants with respect to school Governorships and committee work are taken into account. This committee replaced the ad hoc committee provided for by standing orders, by which the Master, two Senior Wardens and two Past Masters of the Master of the day's choosing, undertook very similar tasks. The point of the change was to ensure greater continuity (and perhaps more transparency) in decision making about office holding.[29] It is worth emphasising, however, that whatever the formalities of the committee structure, the selection of Assistants still relies on a certain amount of accumulated wisdom about the interests and aptitudes of Liverymen, and that the Clerk plays a very considerable role in crystallising that wisdom, and advising the Court on the suitability of applicants.[30]

The Court is in many respects a microcosm of the changing City. Its changing composition in the post-war decades reflects the changes in the City's occupational structure. In the immediate post-war period (1946) the leading occupations (the occupations of nine Assistants are not known) were merchants (six), company directors (five), and lawyers (four solicitors and two barristers). The prominence of the merchants reflects London's role as a mercantile and manufacturing city: there was a cork merchant, an East India Company merchant, a yeast merchant, a timber merchant, a diamond and pearl merchant, and a member described simply as an importer. Groups which were later to be prominent were less well represented: there were two accountants, two stockbrokers, one representative from the world of insurance. There were two clerics, a radiologist (but no other person from the medical professions), just one surveyor, one architect, one engineer, one academic and, most exotically, a royal herald. The larger Court at the turn of the millennium reflects the advance of the financial services sector as the City's mercantile and manufacturing role has contracted: in 2001 there were five accountants, six financial or management consultants, and five representatives of the world of insurance. Nine Assistants sheltered behind the opaque designation of Company Director. The lawyers remain prominent, perhaps more so: there were five solicitors, four barristers, and one marine lawyer. There were three surveyors, two medical consultants, one cleric, and a retired farmer. The Court retains a strong independent school and Oxbridge presence. Of the 15 men holding high office in the Haberdasher years 1997-2002 all were independent-school educated, including three Etonians, two Radleians, two Wellingtonians, and two Marlburians (Stowe, Winchester, and Rugby are represented in this sample by one Haberdasher each). Although six attended Oxbridge (in fact in this sample all Cambridge), the pattern of higher education is more diverse, one each at the London Business School, Nottingham, Durham, London, and (more exotically) Neuchatel; two Assistants attended Sandhurst.[31]

Accumulation of statistical information such as this does not capture the quality of the people comprising the Court. The Company has attracted the services

27   Sir Robin Brook (Master, 1965).

of some notable individuals whose contribution is made the more remarkable by their achievements in other spheres. Let us take three men born within a few years of each other. One of the leading figures in the Company's affairs in the post-war period was Sir Robin Brook (1908-98, Livery, 1932, Master 1965), a star pupil of John Maynard Keynes at Cambridge, and a participant in the British fencing team at the Berlin Olympics in 1936 where he refused to march past Hitler. During the war he became involved in the Special Operations Executive responsible for the secret war behind enemy lines and forging friendships with leaders of the French Resistance. He was recruited by Hugh Dalton to be a left-leaning director of the newly nationalised Bank of England in 1947, and became deputy chairman of the Colonial Development Corporation in 1949. He continued to work for the Secret Intelligence Service until the later 1950s as he established himself in merchant banking. He was Chairman of the Sports Council between 1975 and 1978, and served for 25 years as one of the Special Trustees of St Bartholomew's Hospital.[32] Rather different in experience and temperament was his contemporary, Sir Gilbert Inglefield (1909-91, Livery, 1937, Master, 1971), who survived extraordinary hardships in the war to reach the heights of City office. Trained as an architect, he took an army commission on the outbreak of war, but was taken prisoner by the Japanese after the fall of Singapore. He was set to work on the infamous

28 Sir Gilbert Inglefield (Master, 1971).

Burma-Thailand railway in conditions of such privation that he was reduced to a mere seven stones weight, but his spirit showed in his organisation of his fellow prisoners into a choir to sing Handel's *Messiah*. After the war he worked for the British Council and became director of the family group of light engineering companies. It was in the field of City politics that he was to make his greatest contribution, serving as Alderman for 20 years from 1959, chairing the Barbican Committee from 1963 to 1966 and becoming Lord Mayor in 1967, taking as the theme for his inaugural show 'The return of the arts to the city', reflecting his own long-standing interest in music and architecture.[33] Major-General Sir Jack Bates (1911-91, Livery, 1945, Master, 1978) had joined the Royal Artillery and saw war service in Malaya, Iran, and later Sicily, Italy, and Germany. He enjoyed a succession of commands after the war and was involved in the introduction of nuclear artillery to the British army on the Rhine. In 1964 he became Commandant of the Royal Military College of Science at Shrivenham, and three years later was selected to head the putative tri-services Royal Defence Academy, an effort to provide a university for the services. The project had foundered by 1969 in the face of opposition from the services and mounting costs, and Bates entered a second career, becoming Personnel Director of Thomson Regional Newspapers.[34] It is intriguing that their more controversial contemporary Sir Denys Colquhoun

29   Major-General Sir John Bates
(Master, 1978).

Flowerdew Lowson (1906-75, Livery, 1938) kept his distance from the Company (his main affiliation was perhaps fortunately to the Grocers), never serving in its offices and enjoying only the position of Honorary Assistant from 1951, although attaining the mayoralty; he resigned from the Haberdashers' Court of Assistants in 1963. Free of the Company in 1938, the 'unit-trust whizz kid' of the 1930s, and a colourful Lord Mayor in Festival of Britain year (1950-1), Lowson had a reputation as a man of dubious integrity, always regarded with suspicion by the city establishment ('a bit of a thruster' was how Sir Robert Pearson, former Chairman of the Stock Exchange, described him in 1949), who was found guilty of 'grave mismanagement' by a D.T.I. investigation in 1974.[35]

These biographical vignettes have been introduced to bring to mind the sheer variety of experience on the Court and to underline the importance of getting the right men in place. It is also crucial to the proper functioning of the Court that it should have a balance between those with experience, and those as it were learning the ropes, and that the Court should remain open to those bringing fresh ideas. It has sometimes been a difficult balance to strike. Prior to 1958 it was customary to elect the two junior Wardens direct from the Livery on the principle of seniority, perhaps not the best means of securing the service of men with experience of the Company's business. Indeed David Sime recalls that when he came on to the Court the view prevailed that one should sit quietly for a few years, deferring to the senior members.

A committee to redraft Standing Orders had been appointed in 1952, but it did not produce its final report until 1957. Major changes followed in 1958. It was decided that the Junior Wardens should be elected from Assistants of some three to four years' standing, and arrangements were made to ensure that in the meantime they would become properly acquainted with the Company's business through service on its committees and as School Governor. Service in the Senior Wardenships would follow about ten years after service as Junior Warden. It was also emphasised that the prime consideration in election to office should be suitability and not seniority.[36]

This is essentially the model which prevails today, though other pressures are beginning to suggest themselves. The increasing longevity of Court members has produced in some quarters a sense that perhaps the Court is too 'top-heavy'. Past Masters inevitably enjoy a considerable amount of informal power because of their accumulated experience. Proposals to institutionalise that power, as in the so-called 'Privileges Committee' mooted by Ian Crosse (Livery, 1956, Master, 1982) in 1989, did not prove popular, though the new Membership and Appointments Committee does give two Past Masters a considerable role, albeit one balanced by the current Master and Senior Wardens.[37] In 1999 there were, in addition to the Master and Wardens (five), 18 Past Masters, 18 'ordinary' Assistants, and six Honorary Assistants (excluding H.R.H. The Princess Margaret), a total of forty-seven. The 1999 corporate review proposed (in an interesting demonstration of the importance of seating to the maintenance of hierarchy) that Past Masters should sit apart from the current Master rather than flanking him and that at the age of 75 their voting rights should be reduced to one half vote. This was one of the most controversial elements of the review, and was rejected by the Court, members of which pointed out that in any case votes at Court meetings were very rare. Nevertheless, the discussion does reveal a sense in the Company that the pace of change is not swift enough and that perhaps junior Assistants with important contributions to make are not receiving full opportunities.[38]

Each Haberdasher year is marked by the installation of a new Court of Wardens. Its composition is designed to secure a balance between mid-career Assistants who have already acquired some experience on committees and school Governorships and more senior Assistants on the path to the Mastership. The practice whereby the Master normally serves as Second and First Warden in the two preceding years ensures a degree of continuity in decision making, and enables Masters of a reformist bent to build up a momentum for change. Nevertheless, it must be stressed that the key determinant of a Master's success in pursuing his agenda lies in his ability to 'evolve' change rather than rushing at things and antagonising the rest of the Court.[39]

The theme of the growing burdens on the Master is a constant one. The vote of thanks to the retiring Master, Bernard Elliott (Livery, 1911) in 1957 records that only those who had done the job or had been closely connected with its duties could fully realise what it involved in time and responsibility. Every Court member, however, would appreciate that its practical burdens

30   Publication of Master and Wardens, 1994. From left to right: Mr Richard Hamersley (Third Warden), Mr Peter Bedford (First Warden), Captain Michael Barrow (Clerk), Mr Anthony Pilcher (Master), Mr David Inglefield (Second Warden), Mr David Evans (Beadle), and Mr Tim Jackson-Stops (Fourth Warden).

had vastly increased over the last 50 years. No longer did the Master preside over a smoothly operating organisation which ran by custom and only needed routine attention.[40] Although the later years of the 20th century saw various efforts to reduce the burdens on the Master's time, the expansion in the range of the Company's charitable activities, the concern to gain as much familiarity as possible with the work of the schools, and a more crowded Haberdasher social calendar, has meant that the post continues to demand a great commitment of time.[41]

For instance, in a typical year (2000-1), Brian Shawcross (Livery, 1960) as Master chaired 11 meetings of the Court of Wardens and ten meetings of the Court of Assistants, and commendably chose to attend 40 meetings of committees or school boards, covering the full range of Haberdasher activities. Many of these meetings were preceded by briefings from the Clerk or by the Company's administrative staff. Thirty-six lunches were associated with the Company's committees, and most were hosted by the Master. Each school was as usual separately visited by a deputation, and a further five school speech days and prize-givings attended. Other school events included three school carol services, two sporting fixtures (the Fraser Bird seven-a-sides and the four girls' sports), and the Hatcham Opera. In addition to the three carol services already mentioned, the Master attended 11 church services, including the Millennium Service in St Paul's, the Golden Lecture, the United Guilds Service, and the Company Church Service to commemorate benefactors. Company social events hosted by the Master included the receptions or lunches held after the services just mentioned, three Livery dinners, the young Livery dinner, the Young Haberdashers' Dinner, the Publication Dinner, the Banks Dinner, the Masters' and Clerks' Dinner, as well as three dinners associated with the evening meetings of the Court of Assistants (two) and Court of Wardens (one). The Master also receives a huge variety of invitations to other City social occasions. Brian Shawcross represented the Company at 25 non-Haberdasher evening functions. These included set-piece civic occasions like the dinner to meet the Lord Mayor and Sheriffs and the Mansion House Dinner, as well as more informal dinner parties between the Masters and Clerks of the Great Twelve, which give opportunities for the circulation of ideas. The Fishmongers' breakfast after their tour of Billingsgate market, the Vintners' swan-upping, and the Summer Weekend Ball at the Ironbridge Museum near Telford provide some pleasurable variety to the diet of formal dining among Companies. Other social activity takes the Master beyond the City proper: Shawcross attended three dinners with other guild organisations outside London (the Cutlers' Forfeit Feast at Sheffield, the York Merchant Adventurers' Venison Feast, and the Bristol Merchant Venturers' Feast), and lunched with the Royal Green Jackets (affiliated to the Company), Trinity House, the National Maritime Museum (in recognition of the Company's support) and (at the invitation of the Grocers) the Foundation Appeal for Reed's School at Cobham. Other visits were made to the Lord Mayor Treloar School and College in Hampshire for the disabled (with which the Company has long-standing associations), the Royal College of Art (to which the Company provides an annual prize), the Museum of London, Tate Modern, and the Summer Exhibition at the Royal Academy. For those still trying to run a professional career or a business it can be a gruelling schedule. On 28-31 March 2001 the Master attended a lengthy deputation at Elstree and hosted the Company outing to the new Hall site (28th), attended briefings by the Clerk and Assistant Clerk for Charities, chaired a Court of Assistants meeting, attended the Golden Lecture and hosted the Livery lunch which followed, only to face a dinner at the Mansion House (29th), and attended the United Guilds service and hosted the Livery lunch which followed (30th). Brian Shawcross spent 100 nights in the Master's flat, and was involved in Haberdasher business on 96 days in his year.

As with most organisations of its kind, there is a certain amount of institutional inertia within the Company which acts as a brake on the pace of change and blunts the impact of individual personalities. Most Haberdashers will recognise that there have been individual Masters whose commitment, fertility in new ideas, and forcefulness (in varying combinations) have shaped the Company's direction. Among the more influential Masters, one should number Sir Robin

31 Captain Michael Barrow, Clerk (1983-1995) directing the Master, Mr Bruce Sturgess and Mr Julien Prevett, at Monmouth Girls' School, 1994.

Brook and Dick Liddiard (for their financial acumen), Christopher Bostock (the prime mover behind the Hatcham C.T.C. proposal, and the framer of the so-called Bostock Rules for loans to the schools), Harold Quitman (the architect of the Company's property policy in the key decade of the 1980s), and Sir Brian Jenks (Livery, 1961, Master in 1988 and 1992, for his role over a whole range of Company activity, including the new Hall). Others may have been less innovative, but none can doubt the imprint of their personalities on their periods of office. One thinks of David Sime and Major-General Jack Bates, each a powerful integrating force, extremely popular among members and schools alike.[42]

At the side of every Master stands the Clerk, whose role is critical to the effective functioning of the Company. He is responsible for the preparation of the business of the Court, instructing the Company's advisers, liaising with the School Heads and Bursars, co-ordinating the Company's charitable activities, and running the 'fraternity', ensuring that members are given opportunities to participate and identifying those who might give more. The Clerk also acts as a Personal Assistant to the Master and therefore the personal chemistry between the Clerk and the Master determines the smooth discharge of business. Because the Master changes each year, the Clerk must enjoy not only the normal requirements of a grasp of detail and a sympathetic understanding of the main areas of the Company's activities, but also the ability to get on with a variety of different personalities: he must be made of the willow not of the oak! But the Clerk can come to acquire a considerable reserve of informal power over the years of his service. He is uniquely well positioned to get to know the Livery and therefore to shape the pattern of recruitment on to the Court. The quality of the Assistants therefore reflects in part the judgement of the Clerk.[43]

It is intriguing that whereas the early 20th century had been dominated by the Eagleton 'dynasty' of solicitor Clerks, the retirement of Guy Eagleton in 1950 ushered in a succession of four naval Clerks. Commander Harry Prevett had joined the Royal Navy in 1917, and had become Secretary to Admiral Pridham Wippell in the 1930s. During the Second World War he was based in Alexandria, where Pridham Wippell was Second-in-Command of the Mediterranean Fleet, and was present both at the Battle of Matapan and in H.M.S. *Barham*, Pridham Wippell's flagship when it was sunk with the loss of 800 lives.[44] Commander Bill Miller, who succeeded as Clerk in 1966, had been on Prevett's staff at Plymouth after the war, and was trained as a naval barrister.[45] Captain Michael Barrow came to the Clerkship in 1983 after 37 years in the Navy, culminating in the command of H.M.S. *Glamorgan* (his sixth command) in the Falklands campaign.[46] He was in turn succeeded in 1995 by Captain Robert Fisher, who had commanded three frigates and served in several Ministry of Defence posts before ending his naval career as Commandant of the Royal Naval Staff College, Greenwich.[47] Although all of naval background, these men have all brought their different styles to the office. Bill Miller was a man of words and the custodian of model minutes; Michael Barrow was a self-styled 'man of action', who made it his mission to get to know and to involve the Livery to a greater extent; Robert Fisher sought to further the modernisation of the Company, and bore the brunt of the building and occupying of the new Hall.

Office practices have been modernised in line with developments in the world of business. Michael Barrow talks of the 'three Clerks' regimes': pen and carbon paper under Bill Miller, the word processor under his own regime, and full scale computerisation under Robert Fisher. There is a lot in that. In 1948 Cooper Bros. were consulted about office management, and carbon copies were introduced; a Reorganisation Committee of 1950 set up primarily to deal with estate organisation also made recommendations with respect to filing and minute keeping. It was from 1950 that typed minutes were first produced, but these ran alongside the traditional hand-written version until 1958.[48] The Company purchased its first word-processor in 1983 at what seems an astronomical cost: £2,794.50 and supported by a service contract at £750 per annum; another machine arrived the following year.[49] Full-scale computerisation of the Company's activities was implemented after a review by consultants in 1992-3; the Company acquired e-mail in 1998, and the web-site followed in 2001.[50]

More efficient office practices have not however necessarily reduced the workload on staff, as the range of tasks has expanded. In 1940 the office staff comprised eight people: the Clerk (Guy Eagleton, in the Company's service since 1925, succeeding his father as Clerk in 1931, and salaried at £1,350 per

32   The Company Staff at the handover of Clerks in 1995. Left to right, back row: Miss Elizabeth Fordham, Mr Mick Kelson, Mrs Katharine Holder, Mr David Evans, Mrs Sheila Carlin, Mr Barry Turner, Miss Sanita Kissore; front row: Mr Alan Musk, Captain Robert Fisher, Captain Michael Barrow, Mr Bob Goodwin, and Mr Tim Marsh.

annum), an Assistant Clerk (W.S. Ingram, appointed in 1908 and salaried at £625 per annum), who performed the tasks that would later be associated with the Accountant, and at a more junior level a second Assistant Clerk (J.A. Tait appointed in 1939 on a wage of £5 per week), and a Rent Clerk (A.G. Rumbell, first appointed in 1918, and in 1940 on £5 10s. per week). The office was dominated by Miss M.G.V. Perry, first appointed in 1909, and described as a typist (£4 10s. per week) although she would later have been described as the Clerk's Secretary. There were another two junior clerks (one on £4 10s. per week, the other on £2 per week), while Mrs Tait performed general office duties (£1 10s. per week).[51] Thirty years later in 1970, although titles may have changed, the basic structure was little altered with nine people. Beneath the Clerk was the Accountant (at that time Raymond Bell) and a Property Assistant (Lt Cmdr J. Stedman). The Clerk's Secretary (the formidable Peggy Singleton, 1955-73) and a Book-Keeper (first appointed in 1957, and predecessor to the

Accounts Assistant) provided the key administrative support to these officers, and were assisted by four typists. The main change was that the work of the Property Clerk and the Rental Clerk (keeping the property register, collecting rents, and arranging insurances) had been handed over to the estate managers, Stock, Page, Stock.

By the early 1970s, however, the administration was in some disarray and a so-called 'environmental study', precipitated by the impending retirement of Miss Singleton, was commissioned from Spencer Stuart and Associates in 1973. They emphasised that although the Company could draw on the services of dedicated and long-serving staff, there was a tendency for their responsibilities to grow adventitiously, with apparently random tasks being allocated to individuals: thus the Book-Keeper was responsible for archival enquiries, maintaining the property register, and mailing rent notices. Relations with professional advisers were poorly defined. Under pressure of work Bill Miller had abandoned the practice of written instructions to the advisers with the result that there was potential for duplication and confusion: separate property registers were being maintained by the estate managers and by the Company's own administration. The report concluded that the 'efficient handling of the administrative task has depended more on the ability and dedication of various individuals than on the efficiency of the administrative structure as a whole'.[52]

The main recommendation of the report was the appointment of a Legal Adviser to reflect the increased volume of conveyancing work involved in the management of the Company's property. The Company implemented this with the appointment of Sam Whiteley (1973-6), Barney Whitehead (1976-88) and Walter Greenwood (1988-9).[53] This appointment was an indication of a new trend: a reduction in the size of the clerical staff and an increase in the number of senior administrative posts, which have gradually become more specialised. The number of typists fell from four to three in 1972, and by the 1990s to two. The Legal Adviser gradually began to diversify into other areas of activity (another sign of adventitious development), including acting as Clerk to the Elstree Governors, reflecting the increasing prominence of schools business, and on Greenwood's death he was replaced by a Schools Assistant, the first of which was Adrian Burns, the Project Director for the Hatcham C.T.C. He was succeeded by Tim Marsh in 1991 on Burns' appointment to the post of Bursar of the new C.T.C. Meanwhile the appointment of an Assistant Clerk for Charities (Alan Musk and later Brian Blair) relieved the Clerk's Secretary and the Accountant of much of the routine work of charity administration. By 1999 the need for an additional senior post was felt in part because of the pressures of the new Hall on the Clerk, and an Assistant Clerk for Planning and Development (with responsibility among other things for I.T. developments) was appointed. It will be evident that the resultant structure allows for a degree of specialisation of function at the senior administrative level with individual officers responsible for accounts, schools, charities, and planning, all answerable to the Clerk. This has allowed for more devolution of responsibility from the Clerk, whose role has become that of Chief Executive.[54]

33 Mr A.E.V. Hooke, Beadle (1945-1968) is pictured to the right of a
group including Commander Harry Prevett (Clerk), Mr Edward Dodd,
Mr Charles Gardner, and Mr Richard Blundell, during Gardner's term
as Master (1959-60).

A greater sensitivity towards the interest of the outside world in the Company's
affairs is reflected in the part-time position of Archivist, which began under
Michael Barrow as a one-day-a-week commitment in 1984, but has grown to a
three-day-a-week position. The Archivist's duties extend not only to answering
queries on matters historical but also encouraging knowledge of the Company
among its members and pupils at its schools, and providing advice to the
Fine Arts Committee. The holders of the position have successively been R.K.
Burnett, Helen Bradley (initially employed as the author's research assistant
on the original *History*), and John Cope (Livery, 1958).[55]

The fraternal life of the Company requires a staff which does more than provide
administrative and secretarial support, and here the Beadle and his staff are
critical. The Beadle acts as the Clerk's right-hand man in all matters domestic,
dealing with caterers and contractors, looking after the building including its
security (he is resident on the Hall site), and ensuring the smooth running of
Company ceremonial and functions. For many Company members the Beadle's
Office remains an invaluable point of contact, and over the years Beadles might
come to gain the confidence of Company members, officiating at their weddings
as John Oakman regularly did. Until the retirement of J.C. Haynes in 1975 there
had been an Assistant Beadle, but the post was then dropped until 2002 when
the greater pressure of work resulting from the increased volume of functions
at the new Hall necessitated the revival of the post. The Beadles tend to be

34   Mr David Evans and Mr John Oakman, B.E.M., Beadles, at handover
in the Luncheon Room of old Hall, 1992.

recruited from a military background. John Oakman (1968-1992) had been a
Company Sergeant Major in the Royal Fusiliers, his successor David Evans was
a Royal Navy Chief Petty Officer, the new Assistant Beadle, Eddie O'Shea, a
Sergeant who served with the King's Troop of the Royal Artillery. Under the
Beadles are the two housemen, who perform the invaluable 'back-stage' services,
including the care of the Company's silver and the wine.[56]

Other key relationships in the efficient functioning of the Company are those
with the professional advisers. Some of these relationships have been very
long-standing. The association with Stock, Page, Stock, who acted as surveyors
to the London and Middlesex properties outside the City for much of the
period under review, lasted over 150 years: Henry Stock had been elected
Liveryman of the Haberdashers' Company, and went on to become Company
architect, designing the Victorian buildings at Monmouth School. Dawsons
(who had absorbed the Eagleton firm in 1950) provided legal advice for 150
years.[57] The Company has always sought to maintain a close watching brief
over the work of the advisers. There was an important restructuring of the
relationships between the Company and its surveyors in 1950, when surveyors
were appointed for each of the estates, and it was decided that a single architect
should be appointed for all the schools. This meant relieving T.C. Page of his
involvement with the city properties, including the redevelopment of the Hall
site (which were henceforth the responsibility of A.C. Taylor of Jones, Lang,

35   Annual cricket match against the Company's professional advisers at Elstree, 1984.

and Wootton), and with the school buildings at Newport (to which he had
not been able to give his full attention) and the Aske schools at Hampstead
and Acton (which he was more reluctant to give up).[58] But dissatisfaction was
expressed with the policy of employing one architect for all the schools, and
in 1962 it was decided to allow schools to appoint their own architects from
among local firms.[59] Also in 1962 the Company expressed anxiety about the
performance of its corporate investment portfolio which had been handed
over to Rothschilds in 1957, and after an interview with Evelyn de Rothschild
secured an undertaking from him that he would attend the meetings at which
the Company's portfolio was discussed; the Investments Sub-Committee was set
up the following year to monitor performance.[60] In 1963 the firm of Jackson-
Stops also came under scrutiny in respect of advice it had offered over the
purchase of Aldenham, but the firm was exonerated after further enquiries
by the Court of Wardens.[61] The Company parted company with Dawsons in
1989-90 expressing some doubts about the quality of advice it had received
over the Hall, and legal advice is now provided by Travers, Smith, Braithwaite.
Personal relationships with these firms, and in particular good relations between

36   The Hall Staff in January 2003 in courtyard of the new Hall. From left to right: Mr Aidan
Doyle, Captain Robert Fisher, Mr Peter Eaglestone, Mrs Anja Johnson, Miss Liz Fordham, Mr
Barry Turner, Mr David Evans, Miss Sanita Kissore, Mr Brian Blair, Mr Eddie O'Shea, Miss
Helen Marlow, and Mr Tim Marsh.

the Clerk and the senior advisers, are essential to their smooth working. It
is interesting that although the firm giving the Company investment advice
has changed several times, continuity was provided by the late Christopher
Bomford who stayed with the Company between 1984 and 1998 through the
successive changes of firm.[62]

By way of instancing the importance of the professional advisers, one need
only recall the policy pursued in the 1980s of selling off residential properties
and reinvesting in commercial ones, at which less hard-headed advisers may
have balked. Harold Quitman, though having a professional suspicion of
surveyors and frustrated by what he saw as the conservatism of the senior
partners of Stock, Page, Stock, nevertheless enjoyed extremely good relations
with Christopher Maunder-Taylor, then one of the more junior members of
staff. There were some tensions with Jones, Lang, and Wootton over advice
received in respect of the Bishopsgate properties and Garrard House and, in
dealing with its City properties, the Company switched at the suggestion of

Sir Robin Brook in 1979 to Debenham Tewson and Chinnocks (later D.T.Z. Debenham Thorp, and then D.T.Z. Debenham Tie Leung), whose representative Keith Way enjoyed the confidence of both Quitman and the Clerk. For the commercial properties Quitman brought in Conrad Ritblat & Co. with whose 'cut and thrust' approach he was in sympathy.[63]

The story of the organisation of the Company since the war has thus been one of ongoing modernisation, but one which has sought to retain connections with traditional values. The Company has changed in step with many other City institutions: it is much less 'starchy', much more open to new ideas, and more professional. It remains, however, committed to the distinctive values of fraternity, and it is to the meaning of the Company for its members that we now turn.

Chapter Four

The Company and its Members

Although it lost its connection with the trade of haberdashery in the 17th century, the Company has retained the traditional methods of recruitment – apprenticeship, patrimony, and redemption.[1] Liverymen and, exceptionally, freemen may take young people (their children, friends or relatives, or pupils from any of the Company's schools) as their apprentices; these persons later become free by 'servitude'. By patrimony, those whose father or mother was free of the Company before their birth can claim their freedom. Freedom by redemption enables the Company to broaden its recruitment by taking on individuals nominated by two Company members and approved by the Court of Assistants; it may be bestowed by the Company in recognition of long and loyal service. Members are made free by a great variety of connections. David Sime, an Edinburgh man by birth and upbringing, recalls that he hadn't a clue about the Haberdashers until introduced through William Glover (Livery, 1905, Master, 1949) whose niece Sime married and in whose gas appliance business he worked for 15 years. Gordon Bourne, a young consultant at St Bartholomew's Hospital in 1960, was encouraged to come in by Lord Moynihan (Livery, 1930, Master, 1963) to provide medical advice for the Company's pupils and employees in the interstices of what was then a more flexible Health Service. Harold Quitman's godfather was Bernard Elliott who had always intended to take him as apprentice, but never got round to it, so that Quitman also came in by redemption.[2] Other redemptioners have been recruited specifically for the specialist skills they could bring. Owen Swingland (Livery, 1977, Master, 1987), an expert in tax law, was also an ex-head boy of Hatcham; Michael Wheldon (Livery, 1976, Master, 1999) and Peter Davidson (Livery, 1990) were both invited to join for their knowledge of property.[3]

There is inevitably a strong element of family continuity within the Company, and a few examples will demonstrate the range of kin involved, the strength in some cases of family traditions of service, the variety of talents which can be brought to the Company from individual families, and the social mobility evident within individual families. One family which has produced members in three generations is that of the Jenks. Sir Maurice Jenks (1872-1946) was the son of a Bread Street cabinet maker, who joined the accountancy firm of Isett & Co. as a Clerk at the age of 15, becoming a partner by the age of 24, and taking over the whole business which became Maurice Jenks & Co. in 1896. He pursued a career in the City corporation, was elected a common councillor in 1910 and served as Lord Mayor in 1931-2, after which he was created Baronet of Cheap. He became free of the Company in 1924 and was Master in 1941-2. Sir Maurice's son, Sir Richard Atherley Jenks (1906-93), a partner in the family accountancy business, also held office in the Company, but did not rise higher than third Warden. Both his sons Sir Brian Jenks (b. 1933), a partner with Touche Ross and another accountant, and Peter Jenks (b. 1936, Livery, 1962), a stockbroker, are also Liverymen, and Sir Brian has carried on the family tradition of service in high office with two years as Master in 1988-9 and 1992-3.[4] There have been other families with several members, like the Copes who illustrate the range of professions and interests that might be represented by one kin group. The Revd Anthony Cope (Livery, 1930, Master, 1962) was brought into the Company in 1930 through his kinsman the Revd Canon Thomas Groves Edwards (the Groveses had been one of the Haberdasher dynasties of the 19th century), and he was joined in 1936 by his brother, Sam, a timber merchant specialising in teak from Borneo. Anthony Cope in turn introduced his first cousin, Thomas Cope (the managing director of one of the key wharves in the port of London) to Sir Cullum Welch (Livery, 1948, Master, 1966), and he became free in 1959, joining the Court in 1964, soon after Anthony Cope's Mastership in 1962-3, later resigning from the Court as he wearied of commuting. Sam's son, Charles, a furniture restorer by profession, is a Liveryman (1986). John (Livery, 1959) and Robert (Livery, 1960) Cope, Anthony Cope's cousins, were respectively a schoolteacher who became Company Archivist in 1993, and a builders' merchant. Robert's sons, Andrew (Livery, 1991) and Charles (Livery, 1997), also joined the Company, one carrying on the family business, the other working as a television editor with the BBC. George Pulman (Livery, 1976), a barrister and Assistant, is married to Anthony Cope's younger daughter.[5]

However, the family element is not over dominant, and the dynasties are not deep-rooted in the ways that they are in some other companies. It was estimated that of the 78 men elected to the Livery in the ten years to 1998, 47 per cent had been 'family' (i.e. relatives of other members), 13 per cent 'scholastic' (i.e. from the Company's schools), and 40 per cent 'outsiders' (i.e. persons with no prior connection with the Company).[6] There is, however, reason to suppose that until the later 1960s those with family ties received preferential treatment. In the early 1960s the Company had begun to be anxious about the growing size of the Livery: there had been 288 Liverymen in 1948, there were 320 in 1963.[7] The response to this had been the decision in 1961 that admission by redemption should take place only in very exceptional circumstances, in order that the sons of existing members should not have their chances of Livery prejudiced by interlopers. This short-sighted policy was abandoned in 1963, from which time the self-imposed limit on the size of the Livery of 320 dates. In 1988 the Company reviewed the size of the Livery, and noted that there was a number of inactive members who were subsequently invited to become 'dormant' and no longer invited to Company functions. In 1989 there were 308 Liverymen of whom 34 were dormant. Dormant Liverymen have the right to be restored to active membership if their circumstances change.[8]

It was decided in 1963 that candidates for the Livery should be interviewed by the Court of Wardens and their particulars circulated to all Assistants, prior to the candidates being entertained together; the Court of Wardens was to make the selection, placing otherwise worthy candidates for whom there was not yet space on a waiting list.[9] It is striking that the radical recommendations of a sub-committee on entry to the Company chaired by Sir Robin Brook in 1969 were dropped. There had been criticism from the Corporation about the apparently anachronistic routes of servitude and patrimony, and Brook's committee suggested that apprenticeship should be confined to those genuinely undergoing training at the master's place of business, and argued that patrimony was problematic because it was 'a right irrespective of merit', but reluctantly recognised that it would have to continue: the radical conclusion was that redemption should be the normal method of entry.[10] Redemption is now becoming a more common mode of entry. In the 1980s, when an average of 20 freemen were admitted each year, 23 per cent came in by servitude (that is apprenticeship), 31 per cent by patrimony, and 46 per cent by redemption.[11] In 1970 it was agreed that any member with a tie with any candidate (whether that of blood relative, or acting as an apprentice's master, or as a sponsor for freedom by redemption) should be excluded from the selection procedure altogether, rather than merely withdrawing for the discussion of the candidate in question. The aim was greater transparency, but there is the implication that the exercise of patronage had in the past resulted in the admission of persons of lower calibre.[12] There is now emphasis on competitive entry to the Livery with young Freemen, irrespective of the method of entry, being invited annually to put themselves forward for selection by interview; the fact that the number of candidates exceeds the number of available spaces is taken as, a healthy sign.

What kind of people become Liverymen? They are predictably enough overwhelmingly resident in London and the South-East: no fewer than 68 per cent live in this area, and only 7 per cent reside in the area north of a line drawn from the Severn to the Wash.[13] An analysis of the Company's Livery lists suggests that it is dominated by the professions and the industrial services sector. In 1933 these two groups accounted for 31 per cent and 21 per cent respectively of the 229 active (i.e. non-retired) Liverymen whose occupations were designated on the list of that year. In 1990 the professions accounted for 36 per cent and the financial services sector for 43 per cent. Among the professions the Law has remained prominent: there were six barristers and 22 solicitors in 1933, and nine barristers and 22 solicitors in 1990. The Church has retreated while Medicine has advanced. Whereas 18 clerics wore the Livery in 1933, only four did so in 1990. Within the financial services sector the most notable advance has been that of the chartered accountants and company directors. There were eight chartered accountants on the Livery in 1933, and 18 in 1990; no fewer than 41 Liverymen described themselves as company directors in 1990 as compared with 18 in 1933. But the dominance of the professions and financial services sector is still greater than these figures suggests, because the system of classification used conceals people who might otherwise be allocated to these groups. Thus the 10.5 per cent of Liverymen classed as dealers in

37 Clothing of first Haberdasher Lady Liverymen at Court of Assistants held in Saddlers' Hall, 29 June 1999.

1990 are largely accounted for by underwriters and stockbrokers, and the 7 per cent in the building trades by architects, surveyors, and estate agents. The decline in the manufacturing sector from 13 per cent in 1933 to just 2 per cent in 1990 is in part a mirage produced by the opaque label of company director, but the composition of the Livery reflects a broader transformation in the City away from manufacturing to financial and legal services. Another shift has been the growing presence of members of the teaching profession, largely a consequence of the Company's policy of offering the freedom of the Company to long-serving members of staff of its schools.[14] Some feel that given the importance of the schools in Haberdasher identity more should be done to bring in former pupils. When during the Silver Jubilee of 1977 David Sime decided to take the head boys and girls of each Haberdasher School as his apprentices, some members of the Court expressed disquiet, thinking this would dilute what they called the Company's 'family' atmosphere. Two of those apprentices (James Power, Chaplain of Harrow School, Livery, 1987, and Daniel Hochberg, a barrister, Livery, 1986) now sit on the Court of Assistants.[15] It should be stressed that the Livery contains an immense diversity of other occupations: there is a furniture restorer, a film producer, a film designer, a videotape editor with the BBC, a freelance musician, a journalist, a specialist tour operator, a hotel manager, an arboriculturalist, and several academics including three historians!

The position of women within the Company became anomalous in the later 20th century. While women were being admitted to the freedom in greater numbers, and the role of the Master's wife at Company functions was considerably enhanced, women were excluded from the Livery until 1999. The strength of feeling in more conservative quarters is captured by the reaction to a proposal in 1944 that an honorary freedom be granted to a female representative of the Armed Services: the majority of the Court

38 Ladies' luncheon at Ironmongers' Hall, 2000. Mrs Gina Fisher, Mrs Jean Inglefield, and Mrs Charmian Wheldon are pictured with the wives of Masters and Prime Wardens of some of the Great Twelve.

greeted it with amazement, rejecting it as a 'revolutionary measure', and Sir Maurice Jenks dismissing it as 'incongruous'.[16] However, the numbers of women freemen increased after the Second World War. The freedom was granted on retirement to long-serving Headmistresses like Miss A.F. McDonald, (Monmouth Girls' School, 1934-60), made free in 1960, and Miss Joan Kirby, (Hatcham Girls' School, 1958-75) made free in 1975. A more radical departure was the admission in 1964 of Miss A.R.M. Elliott, the daughter of a Past Master, the first woman to be made free by patrimony since 1806. Two years later, Jane Glover, the eminent conductor and daughter of the Headmaster of Monmouth School, was bound apprentice to the then Clerk, Commander Prevett, the first female apprentice for 150 years.[17] The Company's practice of encouraging the apprenticeship of outstanding pupils from its schools has also brought women into the Company. There was still some unease about women freemen: it was an unstated policy to encourage admissions by patrimony of the daughters of freemen who had no eligible sons, but it was admitted in 1987 that there was in fact no impediment to the admission of daughters even where there was a son.[18] By 1990 the total number of female members stood at 77, that is 12 per cent of the membership. During the five-year period 1994-1998 inclusive, 32 of the 115 persons (28 per cent) admitted to the freedom were women.[19]

The Master's wife plays an extremely important role as 'Mistress'. Although she has no formally institutionalised role, it is clear that she can play a critical part in the Company's affairs, not only at social functions, but also, as many are career women in their own right, in the experience she might bring to school deputations and charitable work. It is interesting that the term 'Mistress' although not to be found in the Company's formal pronouncements has come to have a place in less formal Haberdasher discourse.[20]

The growing prominence of women in the Company's membership, combined with the broader social changes which brought women to greater prominence

39   H.R.H. The Princess Margaret planting an alder tree at the Aldersey Bunbury Primary School as part of the quatercentenary celebrations in 1994, watched by the Master, Mr Bruce Sturgess, pupils, staff, and parents.

in the City and elsewhere, as well as in the governance of the Company's schools, made the question of their exclusion from the Livery (and high office) an increasingly pressing one. Its sensitivity is suggested by the discussions which surrounded the question of making H.R.H. The Princess Margaret an Honorary Liveryman in 1986. The Assistants were 'mindful that conferring this honour upon a lady, albeit a royal personage, would be a break with tradition, which could only add weight to existing pressure to admit ladies to the Livery'.[21] Brian Jenks raised the issue of lady Liverymen during his first period as Master in 1988-9, but informal soundings in the Livery suggested that the admission of women to the Livery would not command majority support.[22] He returned to the matter when Master again in 1992-3, and this time there was a survey of opinion in writing and a thorough discussion at the Court of Assistants in February 1993 at which every member had the opportunity to speak. 17 Assistants were in favour, 15 against, and 6 neutral, suggesting that the proposal would not carry the necessary majority of 'two-thirds of those present and voting'. The proposal was dropped, and it was agreed that the Court would not return to it for four years.[23] The issue was re-opened in 1998, by which time opinion had begun to swing more clearly in favour. Nevertheless, it was a potentially divisive matter requiring delicate handling. Some Court members wanted a postal ballot, claiming that the pace of modern business and frequency of travel necessitated a change in voting procedures for those unable to attend meetings, but this was successfully resisted on the grounds that it might reduce the importance of Court meetings. A survey of the Livery was taken. Of the 15 per cent of Liverymen who responded, 36 were in favour of change, seven against, and two unsure.[24]

The opponents of change used a variety of arguments. They claimed that women were already sufficiently involved through the freedom which enabled them, for example, to serve as school Governors; that there was no evidence that the Company was inefficient; that there was a risk of the character of social events changing so that they became 'husband and wife' affairs; that there were few male preserves left. Against this was the sense that there was a considerable reserve of untapped female talent: 37 per cent of those potentially eligible for consideration as Liverymen in the next five years were women. There was also the problem posed by an all-male institution working in a changed world: how could the exclusion of women be justified to L.E.A.s and school Governors?; might discriminatory policies affect fund-raising opportunities?; could family members be expected to put up with the time devoted by husbands and fathers to an all-male body?; would businesses allow flexibility in work patterns to enable employees to attend company meetings, if they felt the institution to be discriminatory? Some sought to assuage the conservatives by anecdote: one Past Master reported that his attitude had shifted when he woke up one morning to find himself in bed with a Liveryman (his wife enjoyed the Livery in her company)! Others reminded the Court that it would be several years before women would be joining them as Assistants. In the event the Court voted 23 to 8 in favour of change, exceeding the two-thirds majority.[25] The first women were clothed with the Livery in 1999: of the 16 Liverymen admitted in 1998-9, ten were women, a deliberate attempt not to single out just a couple of women at the outset.[26]

It is important to realise that the debate over women on the Livery was articulated in terms of the quality of the Livery. One of the major questions at issue was whether an all-gender Livery would be of better quality. This is to remind ourselves that the Company's health depends critically on attracting people of sufficient calibre and energy to devote themselves and give of their time to its activities. It is a point which must be borne in mind as we turn to look at the benefits of membership in the Company's social life. The Livery Companies often felt in the later 20th century that they were dismissed in the popular imagination as wining and dining societies.

In the years of austerity immediately after the Second World War, the Company's social life embarked upon a slow recovery. At the first Livery Dinner since 1939, in June 1946, the Master, Charles E. Fletcher, spoke of the plans for rebuilding but reminded those present of how the Company had been living off capital. In spite of the constraints, in 1946 and 1947 there was not only a Livery Dinner, but the Court and their wives were invited to the Banks Dinner, and the Masters, Prime Wardens, and Clerks of the other 11 Great Twelve lunched with the Master and Wardens, and the Lord Mayor and Sheriffs were invited to lunch with the Master, Wardens, and Court of Assistants.[27] In 1948 the Company celebrated the 500th anniversary of the grant of its first charter. There was some discussion as to whether the Company could afford to celebrate in style, and some counselled that the celebrations should be deferred. But there was a strong sense that a deferred celebration would lack spontaneity, so the Haberdashers went ahead with a more elaborate form of celebration. On 3 June 1948 there was an afternoon service at St Paul's devised by Canon Edwards (Livery, 1910), a reception with tea at the Guildhall to which representatives from the Company's schools were invited, and a dinner for the Court, Livery, and guests in the Egyptian Hall of the Mansion House in the evening. The Company expressed itself well satisfied with the events which cost £878 (well within the budget of £1,000). The celebrations boosted the Company's confidence and sense of purpose, the presence of so many school children underlining their role in the field of education, and the Bishop of Southwark asserting their long tradition of charitable service in his sermon.[28] This optimism carried forward into the following year when, anticipating an improvement in income levels, the summer Livery Dinner was supplemented by a dance at Ironmongers' Hall to which apprentices within two years of the expiry of their term were also invited. Such hedonism in the years of austerity proved too much for two Liverymen who seriously blotted their copybook and were disciplined by the Court of Wardens for improper conduct – they were suspended from the Livery for one year.[29] Moreover, the financial confidence, which lay behind the 1949 entertainment, was somewhat misplaced, for by the end of the year a rather embarrassed Master had to report to the Court that there was an anticipated deficit of £4,800. The result was that serious consideration was given to scaling down the provision of entertainment, including the proposal that the Banks Dinner and the Livery Dinner should each be held in alternate years. The prevailing view, however, was that the prestige of the Company was at stake, and that Court gifts should be cut in preference to limiting entertainments. Some economies were necessary, however. In 1951 committees were served sandwich lunches, and Court members had to pay £2 towards the cost of guests at the Banks Dinner; in 1952 there was no Livery Dinner.[30]

If 1952 was a lean year for entertainment, the coronation year which followed was one of luxurious celebration. It is often remarked how the accession of Queen Elizabeth II marked the lifting of the gloom of the austerity years, and the judgement appears to hold true for the Haberdashers. The Master was present at the service in Westminster Abbey; other company members witnessed the procession in the 200 seats that had been hired along the route; and the Wardens and Beadle joined other representatives of the Great Twelve in a barge decorated with their banners and coats of arms which joined in the river procession.[31] Originally the Company had envisaged either a Livery dinner or a ball; in the event the Livery got both, perhaps because the vote was tied: 96 for a dinner, 96 for a ball! At a coronation ball held at Ironmongers' Hall on 26 June 1953, 400 members of the Company (including all apprentices over the age of 20) were entertained by Sidney Lipton's Dance Orchestra (hired at a cost of 65 guineas), and enjoyed a supper provided for 27s.6d. per head. Christopher Bostock and his wife recall picking their way through the sleeping revellers in the early hours of the morning after. Later on 15 July a Livery dinner at Mansion House was attended by 380 members and guests. Music was provided by the band of the Royal Regiment of Artillery; grace was sung by girls from Acton School, and the boys of Hampstead School, harking back to the first Elizabethan age, sang madrigals. It was entertainment on a lavish scale appropriate for the second Elizabethan age: the ball cost £1,506 and the dinner £1,338.[32]

Thereafter, as financial constraints eased somewhat, the pattern of entertainment was a Livery Dinner, a dinner for the Masters, Prime Wardens, and Clerks of the Great Twelve, and the Banks Dinner for the Court and ladies; the Livery were also being invited to the Publication Luncheon by the mid-1950s, but the absence of a Hall of their own made it harder to sustain a sense of community among members.[33] So, the opening of the new Hall in Staining Lane in 1956 marked an important landmark in the reinvigoration of corporate life. The first meeting of the Court of Assistants took place in the new premises in May 1956, and the building was officially opened by the Lord Mayor, Sir Cuthbert Ackroyd Bt. on 28 June. The opening was followed immediately by a reception to which 350 were invited, and in later months by three dinners for the Livery and their guests enabling them to gain familiarity with their new rooms. There were separate parties for representatives of the schools and for those involved in the construction of the Hall.[34] As the Haberdashers settled into their new Hall, the number of social functions was expanded with an additional Livery Dinner from 1957, and a Livery reception from 1958.[35] From 1961 the number of Livery Dinners was expanded to three a year in order to enable Liverymen to invite guests (each guest costing three guineas in 1961).[36] Another significant change, and one enabled by greater resources, was the change in timing of Publication from lunchtime to the evening, with the result that another dinner was added to the calendar of events from 1963.[37] There was some scaling down in the provision of entertainment within the dinners, though this may have reflected changing sensibilities rather than the interests of economy. Professional singers were replaced by choirs or orchestras from the Company's schools; the military bands which had provided music in the 1950s were often found to be too noisy in the 1960s, and too expensive thereafter.[38] It was not until 1965 that waitresses (as opposed to waiters) served at Company dinners.[39]

Company catering has always been contracted out to City firms. They have been kept up to the mark with periodic complaints, and by the Company's approach to rival firms. In 1948 the House Committee complained about the quality of lunches, singling out for particular censure the use of artificial vanilla in the sweets.[40] Mr Lindsay R. Ring (later Sir Lindsay Ring, Lord Mayor in 1975) of the illustrious city catering firm Ring and Brymer (Birch's) was summoned before the Court of Wardens to hear complaints in 1962 (shortly before he sold the business for a handsome sum to Charles Forte). Commander Prevett's letter to him explained that 'the vegetables are over-cooked and served not properly strained and in a most unappetising manner, whilst the meat is also over-cooked to a state of toughness which seems to indicate a measure of pre-cooking, but most certainly cooking too far in advance'.[41] After a period of economy measures, a 'senior Liveryman' complained in 1984 about the declining standard of food and entertainment at Livery Dinners, but Harold Quitman argued that the dinners retained a certain 'magic'.[42] A complaint from Geoffrey Fox (Livery, 1955, Master, 1986) about the quality of K and M's catering in 1990 led to approaches to other caterers, but there seemed to be little difference in quality.[43] In 1992 it was noted that the cheeses, salads and fruit provided at luncheons sometimes fell short of the expected standards.[44] During another period of belt-tightening in 1973, after catering costs had risen by 22 per cent in a single year, F.H.W. Bedford (Livery, 1946) had urged that the Company should undertake its own catering, but he was countered by the professional hoteliers Sir George Bracewell-Smith (Livery, 1939) and Sir Ian Bowater (Livery, 1927, Master, 1967), who pointed out that catering was not for amateurs.[45] In 2002 on arrival in the new Hall, the Company decided to generate income from commercial lettings and contracted with a single caterer, Chester Boyd Ltd, for both Company and other events and to market the Hall for use by others.

On its wines, however, the Company has maintained an iron grip, building up one of the most impressive cellars of the Livery Companies through the good stewardship provided by successive Wine Wardens, particularly Sir Robin Brook who served 18 years and Sir Brian Jenks. The Company is fortunate also in being able to draw upon the services of Philip Goodband, Liveryman (1975), a Master of Wine, and professional wine consultant. In recent years the Wine Committee has made regular overseas visits (its members paying their own way), for example to the port houses of the Douro in 1989, to Bordeaux in 1994, to the eastern Loire in 1996, to the Rhone in 1998.[46] An idea of the profile of the Company's drinking habits can be gained by considering annual consumption levels. In the Company year 1952-3, the year of the coronation and at the end of the austerity period (total wine consumption in 1952 had been £865; in 1953 it was £1,669), the Company consumed 20 dozen and 5 bottles of port, 16 dozen and 3 bottles of sherry, 6 dozen and 6 bottles of Madeira, 4 dozen and 5 bottles of red burgundy, 13 dozen and 11 bottles of claret, 3 dozen and 8 bottles of Graves, 7 bottles of sauternes, 21 dozen and 7 bottles of champagne (the previous year it had been just 6 dozen and 9 bottles indicating the impact of the coronation), 13 dozen and 11 bottles of hock, 3 dozen and 4 bottles of white burgundy, 7 bottles of Dubonnet, 9 dozen and 4 bottles of gin, 5 dozen and 1 bottle of liqueurs, 4 dozen and 3 bottles of vermouth, 3 dozen and 9 bottles of brandy, and 6 dozen and 3 bottles of whisky. In 1985 the Company consumed 36 dozen bottles of port, 7 dozen bottles of sherry, 23 dozen bottles of red burgundy, 32 dozen bottles of claret, 6 dozen bottles of Sauternes, 39 dozen bottles of champagne, 23 dozen bottles of white burgundy, 8 dozen bottles of Loire Valley wines, 19 dozen bottles of German Alsace whites, 2 dozen bottles of liqueurs, 2 dozen bottles of brandy, and 16 dozen bottles of spirits. The larger volume in 1985 reflects a more varied social calendar rather than rising levels of per capita consumption.[47]

One area in which Company practice has changed is the treatment of lady guests. Women had not even been invited to the service to commemorate the 400th anniversary of the Hall in 1948; at post-war Publication lunches only the wives of the new and retiring Masters and Wardens were invited. Until 1975 lady guests were expected to watch the Publication ceremony from the rather cramped conditions of the gallery of the Hall, but at least from 1954 they were allowed to lunch with the Court after Publication rather than taking their meal separately, as had previously been the case.[48] The wives of members of the Court continued to be invited to the Banks Dinner, at which the conventional toast was 'our ladies', and they received gifts of posies of flowers or handkerchieves (more recently, to provide a more personal touch, the gifts have been chosen by the Master and Mistress with the advice of the Clerk as to costs, and have ranged from table mats to small pieces of silver).[49] There was, however, mounting pressure for more involvement of ladies. In 1961 the Court of Wardens had decided in favour of lady guests at one of the Livery Dinners, but was overruled by the Assistants. Again in 1964, when the number of Livery Dinners was increased to four, a motion for lady guests at one of them was lost by 14 to 12 votes.[50] By the end of the decade sentiments had softened, and it was agreed that lady guests could be invited to the June Livery Dinner of 1969 as an 'experiment'; the experiment was continued in 1970, and in 1971 it was agreed that their attendance should be regarded a regular feature of the Company's programme. The October dinner, however, remained a bastion of masculinity until 1996.[51]

Company dinners, of course, are not merely a matter of conspicuous consumption. They are a means by which a sense of fraternity is fostered and they are a way in which connections are affirmed and influence extended. A study of the guest list of a key dinner shows something of the way the Haberdashers conceived of their place in the city and the wider world. At their coronation dinner in 1953 they gathered about them an impressive guest list: there were representatives from the City Corporation, headed by the Lord Mayor and Lady Mayoress and including key Corporation officers; the Masters and Clerks of the other 11 of the Great Twelve were invited; the field of education was represented by the Heads and Chairmen of Governors of the Company schools, by Florence Horsburgh, Minister of Education, Sir Cecil Dawes, her legal adviser, and Sir Benjamin Bowen Thomas, the head of the Welsh Department at the Ministry; the services by General Sir John Harding, Chief of the Imperial General Staff, and Admiral of the Fleet Sir Rhoderick R. McGrigor, the First Sea Lord; key City institutions by Mr Walter Barrie, the Chairman of Lloyds, and Sir John B. Braithwaite, Chairman of the Stock Exchange; other professional associations by Sir Gerald F. Kelly, the President of the Royal Academy, Sir Cecil Wakeley, the President of the Royal College of Surgeons, and Sir Dingwall G.C. Bateson, a past President of the Law Society; there were key figures in the local communities with which the Haberdashers

40   Haberdashers' picnic at Derby Day,
mid-1980s.

were involved, Lord Raglan, Lord Lieutenant of Monmouthshire and his wife,
and the Mayor of Monmouth; the wider world was represented by Robert G.
Hooker, the American Ambassador.[52]

Social occasions such as the ones we have been exploring obviously promote
friendships among Company members, and provide points of contact for other
members of the Haberdasher 'family', particularly the schools, but they are also
critical in enabling the Company to foster knowledge of its activities among
the members, and in identifying those who might in due course be suitable
for election to the Court of Assistants. There is, therefore, a strong motive for
having a sufficient number and variety of events which can bring the Company
and its members together, and this objective was strongly pursued in the latter
quarter of the 20th century. In 1970 annual Livery luncheons were instituted
and, as it was proving difficult to ensure attendance by certain members of
the Court, from 1981 these were combined with Court lunches.[53] From 1972
the Livery was encouraged to attend lunch after the United Guilds service at
St Paul's Cathedral.[54] In 1976 Fraser Bird suggested the idea of an informal
evening reception at which Liverymen might get to know each other better.
These events, held twice a year, were initially not well attended: 32 Liverymen
attended the April 1976 reception, 27 the April 1977 one, and only eight in
February 1981. They were nearly abandoned after 1981, but reprieved when
it was suggested that an annual reception with guests might secure better
attendance.[55] The cause of extending the Company's sociability was one with
which the new Clerk, Michael Barrow, feeling that the Company's programme
was too orientated to the benefit of the Court, strongly identified. Additional

41 Haberdashers' visit to St Catherine's monastery in Sinai, 1994.

events were proposed from 1984. Livery receptions were revamped: Liverymen were allowed to bring a guest of either sex, and some of the receptions were to be accompanied by talks on aspects of the Company's activities.[56] New events introduced in 1985 included a lunch on the occasion of the election of the sheriffs, a Derby bus, and an evening reception for young freemen and apprentices to which Liverymen were encouraged to invite one freeman under the age of thirty.[57] The wine tours have already been noted, but Haberdashers ventured still further afield when in 1994 a group of 15 Haberdashers and their wives, with 22 friends visited St Catherine's monastery in the Sinai Desert to pay homage at the resting place of the Company's patron saint.[58] Not all the initiatives were equally successful. The attendance at Livery receptions increased to around 90-100 (falling off in the mid-90s) and were judged a success; the Derby bus was only discontinued in 1992 due to the declining ambience of Epsom Downs on Derby Day, while the enjoyable performances by the drawing room opera company Pavilion Opera introduced in 1989 did not muster quite enough support and were dropped in 1995.[59] Liverymen were also encouraged to participate in the Company's sporting fixtures which were extended with cricket matches against the professional advisers, schools, and other opponents joining the long-standing golfing competitions.[60] Reading the minutes in these years gives one the sense of an institution willing to explore all ideas, and constantly assessing the success of its social initiatives. A proposal to set up a dining club among Liverymen did not find favour, but the Clerk's idea for a Young Liverymen's dinner was followed up, and these became a regular feature of the social calendar from 1989/1990.[61]

42   The monastery of St Catherine, Sinai.

As intended, these initiatives undoubtedly increased the familiarity of Liverymen with each other, and with the Company's work, but another important development was an attempt to make the Company more inclusive of its 400-plus Freemen. From 1986 a Freemen's reception was introduced coinciding with the Company's new service of commemoration and thanksgiving from 1995, the idea of Sir Brian Jenks.[62] Also in 1995 a young Freemen's dinner was held for the first time for all those Freemen younger than 28. It is not held every year, but has proved successful in generating involvement by younger members: in 1997, 60 per cent of those eligible attended the dinner.[63] In 2001 the Young Haberdashers' Dinner, bringing together Apprentices, young Freemen and young Liverymen was instituted. Freemen, of course, are also encouraged to take part in the Company's sporting fixtures, and to attend deputations to the schools. In recognition of the need to bind them still more closely to the Company, and keep them informed of Company activities, it was agreed in 1997 that they should receive the same Company newsletters as the Liverymen.[64] The Company's reception, in particular, shows the potential of the newer events to draw more people in and bring the Haberdasher 'family' together. On 8 June 2000, for example, about 200 members and their guests gathered in the Great Hall of St Bartholomew's Hospital after the Company service. Representatives of the affiliated Armed Services and charities supported by the Company, such as the Treloar Trust, Langley House, and the Royal School of Needlework, were also present.[65] There is no doubt that the greater informality of the occasions also ensures a greater degree of social circulation and exchange of information about the Company and its works.

Although there have undoubtedly been moves in the direction of greater inclusivity and informality, it has been important to the Company that the dignity of its traditions be maintained. It is interesting that immediately after the war there was a sense that Publication ceremonies had become scrappy and undignified; through the minutes runs a concern for the re-establishment of the 'ancient ceremony', and there has been little change in the form of publication since. The crowning of the new Master and Wardens with the traditional garlands remains a key component of the ceremony. Likewise, Livery dinners are still fairly formal occasions, with a procession by the Master and Wardens, the proper sequence of toasts, the National Anthem, and speeches.[66] The spirit of fraternity is maintained in the traditional form through the ceremony of the loving cup, so much part of the Company tradition that during the AIDS scare of 1987, when there were doubts about the disease's mode of transmission and the ceremony was threatened with suspension, the Assistants voted by 17 to 11 to retain the form if not the substance of the ceremony (warnings had to be printed on the menu cards).[67] There has sometimes been tension between the traditionalists and those advocating more informality, and nowhere has that been more evident than over the vexed question of dress at the Company's social events. Senior members now wryly recollect the seemingly interminable (but basically good-natured) arguments over dinner jacket or evening dress that so troubled the Courts of the 1970s. The matter was discussed at length by the Court in 1981. To a proposal for mixed white and black ties events Fraser Bird quipped that it reminded him of the occasion when the Rhodesian Minister of Transport had suggested that cars should drive on the left and lorries on the right. It was agreed that the spring and summer Livery dinners should be black tie, leaving the October (men only) dinner as an evening dress occasion but thereby, as opponents pointed out, preventing the ladies from seeing a full dress occasion, and there were several attempts to reopen the issue culminating in a postal referendum of the Livery at the end of 1984 with a view to making the March Livery Dinner an evening dress occasion: 74 voted for dinner jacket and 65 for evening dress. So, the October dinner alone remained white tie.[68]

As the guest lists at its dinners indicate, the Company is concerned not to appear too introverted, using its sociability to strengthen the links with its schools and charities, as well as reinforcing its position within the Establishment. There is no doubting the Company's alignment with the Establishment. Although, in common with other City institutions, the Haberdashers have been willing to adapt to the changing environment of the later 20th century, they also have a strong sense of their historic ties with the Church and the Crown. Their position has often been stated in school speech days. Sir Cullum Welch, in his mayoral year in 1957, told the pupils at a Monmouth prize-giving to adhere

43   Interior of St Lawrence Jewry church prior to a mayoral election on Michaelmas Day.

to three maxims: 'Fear God, honour and pay allegiance to the Queen, and obey your parents'. Likewise, at their dinners Haberdashers are urged to uphold the powerful Trinity of 'the Church, the Queen, and the Worshipful Company of Haberdashers'.[69] The key ritual of the 'Publication' of the new Master and Wardens, at which authority is transmitted within the Company, is followed by a church service held since 1958 in the guild church of St Lawrence Jewry reconstructed after the Second World War, its inner doors paid for by the Company, and incorporating a window to St Catherine, the Company's patron saint. (During the Company's exile from the Staining Lane site use had been made of the Vintners' church of St James Garlickhithe.)[70] In 2002 the Publication service was relocated to the wonderful Norman church of St Bartholomew the Great near the new Hall in West Smithfield. Other key church services are the United Guilds Service in St Paul's (at which all Livery Companies are represented) and the Golden Lecture (endowed by the Jones Lectureship Charity and open to the public), and the Company ensures its presence at the carol services associated with its schools. The Company has the right of presentation (in some cases shared) to a number of livings, some deriving from gifts of advowsons by 17th-century benefactors, others reflecting church building by the Jones Foundation in the 19th century on the Hatcham and Hoxton estates.[71] Since 1995 the Company has held an annual service to commemorate its benefactors and to remind members of the essentially christian nature of the Company. The Company maintains an Honorary Chaplain, in the years after the war an appointment in the gift of the Master each year, but since 1974 a post associated with the Vicar of St Lawrence Jewry (successively The Rev. Basil Watson and, since 1986, The Rev. Canon David Burgess).[72] There has been an effort to foster further links with the Church through granting a senior cleric the status of Liveryman Honoris Causa. The Rt Hon. and Rt Rev. Michael Ramsey (1904-88; Archbishop of Canterbury, 1961-74) was granted this honour while still Archbishop of York in 1959; on his death in 1988, there was a hiatus before the honour was accepted in 1995 by the Rt Rev. Michael Baughen, formerly Vicar (1970-75) and Rector (1975-82) of All Souls Langham Place, and at the time of his nomination Bishop of Chester.[73] Interestingly, although the Company has been willing to use the Golden Lectures to hear persons from different faiths, even issuing an invitation to Pope John Paul II on the occasion of his visit in 1982, the Company is aligned with the Church of England, and a suggestion that Cardinal Basil Hume be considered for the status of Honorary Liveryman in 1992 did not find favour.[74] Nevertheless, some members have from time to time expressed their frustration with the Church of England, one Assistant suggesting in 1973 that Robert Runcie who had agreed to give the Golden Lecture should take as his theme the permissive society, 'against which the Church had so far failed to take a strong line'.[75] We are not in a position to make windows into Haberdasher souls to ask for how many religious conviction is a serious matter, but as we shall see in chapter 6, for several Assistants the issue of religious education in the schools was one on which they felt strongly, and it is from their concerns that the practice of distributing King James' bibles to all pupils at the schools derives.[76] One of the highlights of the Millennium year was a service at St Paul's Cathedral on 24 November 2000, presided over by the Rt Hon. and Rt Rev. Richard Chartres, Bishop of London, and attended by 1,630 people, including H.R.H. The Princess Margaret, School Governors, Heads, staff, pupils, and parents, a key moment for expressing the solidarity of Haberdasher purpose and inscribing a view of a shared christian heritage. This was the last Haberdasher event at which Princess Margaret was present before she died on 9 February 2002.[77]

The ties with the Crown are well developed. The National Anthem is always sung at Publication church services and at the dinner which follows; some of the schools were ticked off in 1995 for not including it prior to school concerts and other appropriate school occasions. All dinners include the loyal toast. As one of the Great Twelve, the Haberdashers have contributed to their gifts which have marked key royal events. In 1947 the marriage of H.R.H. The Princess Elizabeth and Lieutenant Philip Mountbatten was marked by the gift of a mahogany settee, four chairs, and a serpentine-fronted chest of drawers;

when Prince Charles married Lady Diana Spencer in 1981 the Great Twelve presented a George III carved gilt mirror.[78] But in keeping with the later 20th century philanthropic monarchy, other royal anniversaries have been marked by donations to charities of which the royals are patrons: thus Princess Margaret's 60th birthday was marked by a donation of £6,000 to the Horder Centre for Arthritics, and the Queen Mother's 80th by a gift of £1,000 to a charity of her choice.[79] The Silver Jubilee of 1977 was marked by joining with the Great Twelve in the river pageant (admittedly in a decidedly unimpressive barge), the display of coats of arms of the companies on lamp posts outside the Royal Exchange (the Haberdashers' was bent, an oversight corrected by the Corporation after representations from the Company!), a gift shared with the Great Twelve of a new carpet for the Garter Throne Room at Windsor, and the Company's participation through the loan of plate in an exhibition, 'The City and the Crown' at the Guildhall.[80] For the Golden Jubilee in 2002 the Great Twelve paid for a stained glass window in the Chapel Royal at St James' Palace dedicated in November 2002 in the presence of H.R.H. The Prince of Wales.[81]

In common with other City Companies the Haberdashers have sought to strengthen their connections with the monarchy and to gain additional patronage resources through the granting of the honorary freedom to a key member of the royal family. Between 1873 and 1942 the connection had been provided successively by Queen Victoria's third son, Arthur, Duke of Connaught and Strathearn (1850-1942), and his son Prince Arthur of Connaught (1883-1938), who was Master in 1935 to mark King George V's Jubilee.[82] The Haberdashers had approached Princess Margaret in 1954 but the Queen Mother appears to have counselled against the association at that stage. In 1966, however, another approach, this time successful, was made, and she was admitted to the freedom on 1 May that year, later attending the Banks Dinner.[83] The Company was extremely pleased with the level of support it received from Her Royal Highness. She regularly visited the schools, including the opening of Elstree Girls in 1974, and the centenary celebrations at Hatcham in the following year; she saw the Company at work through occasional attendance at committees, and attended several dinners, including for the first time in 1995 a Livery Dinner.[84] From one Haberdasher engagement a year in the early years of her association, her commitment rose to two events per annum through the 1980s, although her subsequent ill-health inevitably meant that she was seen less regularly at Company events.[85] In 1986 after 20 years' association with the Company she accepted the position of Assistant Honoris Causa.[86] The royal connection brought enhanced prestige and valuable publicity for the Company's affairs, but Her Royal Highness appears to have derived real pleasure from her visits especially to the schools. It is true, of course, that Clerks soon learned that visits would go more smoothly if a 'Bearer of the Royal Ashtray' was on hand! In her association with the Company the mask of royal formality sometimes slipped, whether relaxing over tea in front of a blazing fire in the Newland Lecturage House after a whirlwind tour of the

44 Admiral Sir Henry Pridham Wippell.

45 Field Marshal Sir Harold (later Earl) Alexander.

Monmouth schools, or leading the assembled company from the piano in a rendition of 'Smoke gets in your eyes' after a Court dinner at the Hall.[87] The benefits of the royal association are such that the Company was keen to secure a new royal patron. It was delighted when on 20 July 2004 H.R.H. The Earl of Wessex was admitted as a Liveryman Honoris Causa.

Ties with the Armed Services have strengthened. As the Second World War drew to a close the Haberdashers, a high proportion of whom had seen active military service, felt the need to honour key figures in the military, and one was selected to represent each of the Services in the status of Honorary Liveryman. The recipients of this honour were Field Marshal Sir Harold Alexander (1891-1969), later Earl Alexander of Tunis, Marshal of the Royal Air Force Sir Arthur William Tedder (1890-1967), later first Baron Tedder, and Admiral Sir Henry Pridham Wippell (1885-1952).[88] Alexander had been in charge of the evacuation from Dunkirk, being on the last motor launch to leave; as commander in the Middle East from August 1942 he had been able to turn the tide against the Germans in North Africa in the Tunisian campaign of the following year, thereafter commanding the invasion of Sicily and Italy, brilliantly co-ordinating a motley multi-national force, eventually becoming Supreme Allied Commander in the Mediterranean theatre.[89] Tedder had been in charge of Hurricane and Spitfire development between 1938 and 1940, and assumed command of the R.A.F. in the Middle East between 1941 and 1943; he was Deputy Supreme Commander Northern Europe under Eisenhower from the end of 1943, in which he demonstrated the virtues of co-operation

46 Air Chief Marshal Sir Arthur William
Tedder, later First Baron Tedder.

47 Clothing of H.R.H. The Prince Edward, Earl of Wessex, as a Liveryman Honoris
Causa in July 2004.

between airpower and land forces.[90] Pridham Wippell had also served in the Mediterranean theatre; he was Second-in-Command of the Mediterranean Fleet between 1940 and 1942, although his subsequent career seems to have suffered from Churchill's annoyance at the conduct of the Tripoli campaign of 1942, and he spent the rest of the war as Flag Officer at Dover.[91]

Since the death of Earl Alexander, the Army slot has been filled in turn from 1969 by Field Marshal Sir Geoffrey Baker (1912-80), Chief of the General Staff from 1968 to 1971, from 1984 by General Sir Peter Hunt (1916-88), a former Commander in Chief of the British Army of the Rhine (1970-3) and Constable of the Tower of London (1980-85), and from 1990 by General Sir Edward Burgess (b. 1927), Deputy Supreme Allied Commander Europe from 1984 to 1987. When Tedder died in 1967, he was succeeded by Marshal of the Royal Air Force Sir John Grandy (1913-2003), Commander of 249 Squadron in the Battle of Britain, later Chief of the Air Staff (1967-71), Governor of Gibraltar (1973-8), and Constable and Governor of Windsor Castle (1977-88). Following Pridham Wippell, Admiral Sir Guy Grantham (1900-92), after a distinguished war career, Commander-in-Chief in the Mediterranean (1954-7), Commander-in-Chief Channel and South North Sea (1957-9) and Governor of Malta (1959-62) represented the Royal Navy; he was succeeded in 1994 by Admiral Sir Richard Thomas, a former Black Rod, who took his place in 1994, but died two years later. Vice-Admiral Michael Gretton, Chief Executive of the Duke of Edinburgh's Award scheme, and Lieutenant-General Sir Hew Pike, Chief Executive of GAP, became Liverymen Honoris Causa in 2004, thereby continuing the service connections, but with increasing emphasis on the post-military activities of the honorands, particularly their activities in support of youth.[92]

In 1937 the Company began its association with the Queen Victoria Rifles, and the relationship continued when they amalgamated with the Queen's Westminsters to form the Queen's Royal Rifles in 1961, later to become the Royal Green Jackets.[93] In 1984 the Company affiliated with the Queen's Regiment, already closely associated with the Elstree C.C.F. In 1993 the Queen's Regiment was amalgamated with the Royal Hampshires to form the Princess of Wales' Royal Regiment with its headquarters in Canterbury.[94] The Company affiliated with the recently commissioned (July 1986) H.M.S. *Brave* on 17 December 1986. After H.M.S. *Brave* was decommissioned in 2000, a victim of the Strategic Defence Review, the Haberdashers formed a new association in 2002 with H.M.S. *St Albans*, then the Royal Navy's newest frigate, handed over to the Navy in November 2001.[95] In 1992 R.A.F. No.XIII Squadron, then a Reconnaissance Tornado squadron based at R.A.F. Honington in Suffolk, accepted an affiliation, thereby giving the Haberdashers a connection with each of the Armed Services.[96] The Company's links have taken a variety of forms, which can best be appreciated by the nature of the contacts in one year, that of 1993-4 when Bruce Sturgess (Livery, 1970) was Master. A contingent of officers and ratings from H.M.S. *Brave* was entertained to lunch before the ship's deployment to the Adriatic to act in support of the U.N. forces

48 H.M.S. *Brave.*

in Bosnia. There were visits by the Master and others to the Fifth Battalion of the P.W.R.R. stationed at Canterbury and to the First Battalion then on duty in Northern Ireland. Sturgess also attended the Annual Inspection and Prizegiving of the Frimley and Camberley Cadet Corps, whose recently retired Commandant, Brian Gould, had been admitted to the freedom of the Company earlier in the year. There was also the golfing competition against the P.W.R.R. Although No.XIII Squadron was not visited, nevertheless their Commanding Officer, Group Captain Steve Dalton, attended the October Livery Dinner.[97] It is typical of the pattern of reciprocal entertainment which characterises the relationship, familiarising a new generation of Haberdashers who have not seen military service with the activities of the Armed Services. Members of the affiliated units are invited to the Company Service and Reception, and senior officers appear at Livery dinners; special Services dinners were held in 1988, 1991, and 1996. In recent years, Haberdashers have been invited to participate in the P.W.R.R. sailing week. Sometimes Company members have been taken far afield as when a group visited 3 Queens in Cyprus where they were stationed in 1990, or when four Liverymen sailed in H.M.S. *Brave* to the Canaries in 1997.[98] In 1989 the Company instituted an annual trophy (a biscuit barrel in the shape of a ship's bell), the 'Haberdasher Brave of the Year' award for the officer or rating deemed by the Commanding Officer to have made the greatest contribution to the overall welfare of the crew. The trophy was appropriately renamed 'Martyr of the Year' when the new relationship with H.M.S. *St Albans* was created.[99]

49   Affiliation ceremony for R.A.F. No.XIII Squadron, 1992.

Church, Crown, the Armed Services – and of course the City; the Company's fortunes have been closely connected with the City of London through 700 years of Haberdasher history. By the early 16th century the Haberdashers had emerged as one of the Great Twelve Livery Companies entitled to precedence in City ceremonial. Although some of the so-called 'lesser' companies are in fact wealthier than some of those in the Great Twelve, the latter retain a distinctive role in the life of the City. There are a number of social events

50   Mr Geoffrey Fox (Master, 1986) entertained by the Queen's Regiment.

51   Mr Anthony Miller ready for action with R.A.F. No.XIII Squadron.

52   The Master, Mr Bruce Sturgess, in britska of the Great Twelve at the
Lord Mayor's Show, November 1992.

which bring them together (like the Masters', Prime Wardens' and Clerks'
dinners); they play a role on state occasions; and their Clerks meet together
regularly to discuss matters of common concern such as relations with the City,
public relations, and taxation. Perhaps the result has been a culture rather more
inward looking than is appropriate in the modern world. There have been
periodic attempts by groups within the City to foster relations with equivalent
European institutions. Reactions have varied: the Haberdashers' minutes note
in response to encouraging noises from the Lord Mayor on this theme in
1977 that it would be 'only an expensive means of mutual entertainment'. The
main problem, however, seems to have lain in finding equivalent institutions.
In 1999 there was talk of linking up with the Scuole Grande of St Roch in
Venice: the Assistants noted with some perception that the 'only comparison
might lie in antiquity'.[100]
   The Haberdashers are also enmeshed in the structures of City governance
for the Livery enjoy the right of election of the Sheriffs who continue to be
elected by 'open outcry' at Common Hall. The Company has continued to
participate in the key civic ceremonial of the Lord Mayor's procession, albeit
with mixed results. A nadir came in 1956 when Haberdashers were made
to stand in aluminium sentry boxes as 'Guardians of Tradition', in a show

53 Mr Nigel Branson (Sheriff, 2000).

whose theme was the history of aluminium![101] In the interest of greater dignity the Great Twelve agreed in 1961 to contribute to a britska bearing plaques of the crests of the Great Twelve in which four of the Masters and Prime Wardens might ride each year.[102] Haberdashers continued to participate in the City Corporation in the post-war years, providing Lord Mayors in 1947-8 (Sir Frederick Wells), 1950-1 (Sir Denys Lowson), 1956-7 (Sir Cullum Welch), 1967-8 (Sir Gilbert Inglefield), and 1969-70 (Lt Col Sir Ian Bowater). Others have played an important role. Sir John Welch (Livery, 1955, Master, 1990) served as a Common Councillor and chaired the City's Property Committee; David Inglefield (Livery, 1956, Master, 1998) was Sheriff in 1980. There has, however, at the time of writing been no Haberdasher Lord Mayor for over thirty years. As early as 1984 the Court of Assistants was expressing concern about the lack of interest among the Livery in the succession to the mayoralty: they followed up by seeking to remind Liverymen of their responsibilities, and to encourage their participation in ward clubs. Nigel Branson (Livery, 1970), a member of the Court of Assistants since 1990, stood for Sheriff in 2000, and his successful candidacy was accompanied by another drive in civic consciousness raising among the Haberdashers.[103] Branson's willingness to get involved remains untypical, and the lack of Haberdasher participation was

54 Mr David Inglefield (Sheriff, 1980).

symptomatic of a general retreat from the Corporation by the Great Twelve. By
1992 only three Aldermen and three Common Councilmen were from among
the Great Twelve, and in the following year the Clerks of the Great Twelve
expressed anxiety about the calibre of some of those in line for succession to
the mayoralty. Indeed by the early 1990s the Great Twelve, who one might
otherwise consider bastions of corporate conservatism, were putting pressure
on the Corporation to engage in long overdue reform. They have encouraged
(informally) the City Corporation in its measures of franchise reform. The City
of London (Ward Elections) Bill was presented to Parliament in November
1998 and received its final reading in the House of Lords in October 2002.
It is designed to increase the business vote from 16,000 to 32,000 by allowing
limited companies (hitherto unrepresented) to nominate electors according to
the number of their employees while protecting the rights of the 7,100 city
residents.[104] Parallel with these political changes, there has perhaps been some
reduction in the level of social interaction. In the 1960s, the Lord Mayor
endeavoured to attend one Livery dinner a year, by 1970 his attendance was
every other year but has now reverted to every year; in 1994 the Great Twelve
complained about the reduction in the number of their invitations to Mansion
House affairs. Nor does the Lord Mayor appear as regularly at speech days in

the Aske schools. These changes perhaps reflect the growing internationalisation of the Lord Mayor's role as an ambassador for London, the world city.[105]

The Company's associations with the Church, the Crown, the Armed Services and the 'old City' have encouraged some to depict it as a bastion of reaction. Add to that the reputation for 'wining and dining', and one has the makings of a potentially powerful critique. Indeed there have been times in the last fifty years when the Company has reflected on its image problem. In 1965 a highly critical *Panorama* programme about Livery Companies in general (though not the Haberdashers in particular), and a Labour government which was undoubtedly cool towards the City (although Harold Wilson was to dine at the Hall as guest of Sir Cullum Welch in October 1967) stung the Great Twelve into active thinking on the subject. A supplement to *The Times* was considered, but wisely rejected as preaching to the converted; there was serious talk of making a film, but although the Haberdashers seemed enthusiastic there was by no means universal support among the Great Twelve (seven opposed it), and there were some revealing discussions about the means by which 'equal time' could be secured for the Twelve.[106] The Haberdashers have themselves taken modest measures to correct popular misapprehensions. It is interesting that, when planning their participation in the Lord Mayor's procession in 1980 when David Inglefield was Sheriff, they noted the risk of offering too historical an emphasis, and determined to stress a 'positive and up-to-date role', taking as their theme Education and Training, and coralling 130 Haberdasher pupils and their teachers on to a float.[107] In 1985 the Court of Wardens noted that there was a need to make the public more aware of the charitable and other work done by Livery Companies. They noted that 'the overall objective would be to paint a picture of a caring, charitable organisation rather than the wining and dining image which the public normally choose to associate with Livery companies.[108] Thus there has been an effort, perhaps hesitant and faltering at first, but of late more insistent, to bring knowledge of the Company's activities to a wider public. From the early 1960s the Hall was open to the public on four days a year; there have been regular school visits; and the Company's closer involvement with its charities is indicated by more invitations to Company functions to their representatives.[109] The employment of an Archivist from 1984 has enabled the Company to be more responsive to enquiries from the general public. A *Brief History* by Commander Prevett already existed, but there was a sense that something more substantial was needed. They supported Ned Goddard who offered to write the Company's History in his retirement from the Headship of Hatcham Boys' School in the 1960s (a sub-committee was set up in 1965 to manage it), but it was a project he had to give up in 1968 through ill-health.[110] A *History* was eventually produced by the present author in 1991 under the guidance of the so-called Historiographical Committee, realising a long-held ambition of Commander Miller and several members of the Court. The History was supplemented by a brochure drawing attention to the Company's activities in charity and education.[111] The Company was an enthusiastic participant in the exhibition at the Guildhall in July 1989 to celebrate the 800th anniversary of the mayoralty and in the Livery Companies' exhibition also at the Guildhall and visited by 10,000 people five years later. On this latter occasion the Company's stand designed by two sixth formers from Haberdashers' Monmouth School for Girls stressed its role in education.[112]

It is in its sociability that the Company shows the greatest continuity with its original functions. The Livery Companies originated as associations of people with common interests joining together for social and pious purposes; involvement in trade regulation came later. At the heart of the original fraternity's corporate life was the annual mass, commemoration of deceased members, and feast. The Publication ceremonies which combine common worship, eating together, and the renewal of the Company's governing body are therefore in direct continuity with its founding principles. The forms in which it is expressed may have changed, but the essential commitment to the values of 'fraternity' remains constant. Another core value of the early guild was 'charity', concentrated at its outset on the body's own members. Because of the changed composition of its own membership, and because it has become the custodian of key charitable bequests, the forms in which charity is expressed have changed radically too. It is to the Company's role in charity and education in the later 20th century that we now turn.

Chapter Five

The Company's Charities

The structure of charitable activity by the Haberdashers in the later 20th century was to a considerable extent determined by the actions of donors in the 17th century, for the bulk of the Company's key charitable endowments were received in the 150 years after the Reformation. Thomas Aldersey (d. 1597), who established the school and lectureship at Bunbury in Cheshire, was the first of the major donors, but he was soon followed by others. The most generous was William Jones (d. 1615) who had endowed a complex of charities on the Welsh border: there was a school, almshouses and a lectureship in Monmouth, and more almshouses and another lecturer at Newland in the Forest of Dean in Gloucestershire. He had also provided pensions for the Company poor and a lecturer at St Bartholomew Exchange in the City of London. William Adams (d. 1656) founded a school and almshouses at Newport in Shropshire. Robert Aske (d. 1689), a silk merchant, left funds for what became the hospital at Hoxton where 20 old men were to be accommodated alongside the sons of freemen who would be educated there. John Banks (d. 1720) left the Company substantial properties which were to support the relief of their poor. There were also numerous smaller trusts: it was fashionable to leave sums of money to provide loans to young tradesmen, the interest from which might support some other charitable object like the education of scholars at the universities, or annuities to the poor; others like Robert Boddington (d. 1700) and Edmund Boulter (d. 1702) left the Company money to buy property subject to charitable payments. The bulk of the Company's advowsons (rights of presentation to church livings) were likewise the result of benefactions in this period: Lady Mary Weld (d. 1623) had left a fund of £2,000 from which the rectories of Leiston in Suffolk, Wigston Magna, Bittesewell, and Diseworth in Leicestershire, Albrighton in Shropshire, and Chertsey in Surrey were purchased. A bequest from Edmund Hammond added the rectory of Awre in Gloucestershire to the Company's ecclesiastical patronage.[1]

The fortunes of these charities were shaped both by economic factors and by the motives and activities of 19th-century reformers. By 1957-8 the surplus income available for charitable expenditure on the Jones, Aske, and Adams charities amounted to £39,223, £15,728 and £2,640 respectively.[2] Adams was very much the poor relation. The Aske and Jones charities had benefited from lucrative housing developments on their estates at Hoxton and Hatcham, whereas the Adams charity was funded by the manor and woods of Knighton in Shropshire, which being agricultural land did not increase as much in value as the metropolitan estates.[3] Likewise, the fortunes of the 'minor charities' (as they were called for much of our period) varied according to the method of

55   The Jones almshouses at Newland. Visit by the Master, Sir Brian
Jenks, Lady Jenks, the Clerk and Mrs Barrow, who are pictured with the
Lecturer, the Rev. R.H. Parsonage C.F. Rtd., 14 June 1989.

their funding. The value of the loan stocks was eroded by inflation, and in
any case many were lost through the failure of the principal or the sureties in
the later 17th and 18th centuries. Some Company properties had to be sold in
the difficult years after the Great Fire, resulting, in some cases, in temporary
default in charitable payments by the Company. By the early 19th century
payments to the charities on which the Haberdashers had defaulted had been
restored, government securities being purchased to the appropriate values to
maintain the donors' wishes, but the value of the annuities had often been
seriously eroded in real terms.[4] Other charities which had been supported by
modest properties at their inception saw their income swell as they partook
of rising metropolitan property values. By the mid-1950s income from some
of the so-called minor charities was sometimes on a more substantial scale:
Roger Jeston's charity received £2,129 per annum, Boddington's and Boulter's
£898 per annum, William Bond £521 per annum, William Cleave's £463 per
annum, and Throckmorton Trotman's £2,763 per annum.[5]

   The other conditioning factor was the intervention of the Charity
Commissioners (and in the 1870s the Endowed Schools Commissioners) who
were empowered to vary the terms of historic trusts to make better use of their
resources. Thus the Haberdashers' major trusts had been subjected to sweeping
overhauls in the later 19th century. By a scheme of 1873 Aske's Hospital was
closed and the resources of the charity used to establish new schools at Hoxton
and Hatcham, which operated from 1875. At Hatcham the boys and girls had
initially shared the Telegraph Hill site, but its cramped nature necessitated
the acquisition of the Jerningham Road property and the establishment of

56 The Jones almshouses at Monmouth. Visit by the Master, Sir Brian Jenks, and Lady Jenks pictured with the Warden, the Rev. G.H. Coldrington, R.N. Rtd., and pupils from Monmouth School for Girls, 6 July 1989.

the girls' school there in 1889. The school buildings and site at Hoxton were sold to the London County Council in 1898 and, by a new scheme of 1900, a boys' and girls' school were opened at West Hampstead and Acton (the so-called 'northern schools') respectively to join the two Hatcham schools. The Aske schemes had allowed for the payment of £1,500 per annum for general charitable purposes, and these were further defined by yet another scheme of 1918, under which two-thirds were destined for poor freemen and their widows and children, and the residue for medical and other charitable purposes.[6] The Jones charity had escaped major reform in 1868, but in 1891 it was agreed that there should be another three schools (in addition to the existing Boys' School at Monmouth), each of which would receive a block grant from the charity: a Girls' School for scholars and boarders and an elementary school in Monmouth, and a school for scholars and day boarders in West Monmouthshire (eventually established in Pontypool). Another tranche (£1,500 per annum) of money was allocated to the almshouses and their lecturers. But from the Haberdashers' point of view the most vexing feature of the reform schemes for the Jones charity was the stipulations for the application of the residue of the income: the Welsh Intermediate Education Scheme of 1894 had directed the Company to make a capital grant to fund the Monmouth Agricultural School, but that the residue of the income after the payments under the 1891 and 1894 schemes should be given to Monmouthshire County Council, with the proviso that the Council might make top-up grants to the Haberdashers' schools. The scheme of 1910 required the charity to make regular payments to the Agricultural College at Usk, and left the County Council with considerable

57 Vicars of Bunbury pictured with their bishop. From left to right: Rev. Timothy Atkins, D.S.C., Rev. Canon Maurice Ridgway, Rt Rev. Michael Baughen, Bishop of Chester and later Liveryman Honoris Causa, Rev. Canon John Bowers, and Rev. Donald Marr.

discretionary power over the residual income, though it was later agreed that, of the final residue, one-third should go to the Monmouth schools, one-third to the West Monmouthshire School, and the remaining one-third for general educational purposes in Monmouthshire.[7]

Less altered because lacking the swelling resources of the Aske and Jones trusts were the Adams and Aldersey charities. Bunbury School was placed under the inspection of the Committee of the Privy Council for Education in 1863, while in 1898 the lectureship was consolidated with the vicarage to produce one benefice.[8] The scheme for Adams of 1878 altered the structure of governance and revised the various sums payable, while that of 1909 recognised the separation of the school from the eleemosynary charity (supporting the almshouses) which had been established three years previously, and provided that the whole income should go to the school managers after the eleemosynary payments.[9]

The 'minor charities' were also subject to the intervention of the Commissioners, the schemes often being slightly varied to give the Company more discretion. Thus, William Cleave had left money to the poor of the Company; by a scheme of 1876 the forms of that relief were specified as pensions, provision for the education of their children, and their support in convalescent or other hospitals, but the Company was allowed to employ any residual income on deserving poor persons not being free of the Company, but resident in London.[10] By a scheme of 1921 the Company was authorised to consolidate some of the very smallest charities directed to its own poor. Their combined income, at that date £181 14s. 0d., was applied according to the terms established for the scheme of 1918 for the regulation of Aske's eleemosynary charity.[11]

The legacy of the charitable activities of previous generations of Haberdashers has been a very varied portfolio of activities. Critics of the Livery Companies sometimes allege against them the high overhead cost of administering a large number of small charities, but such criticisms fail to recognise two points. First, the Company is very much constrained by the terms of the trusts it administers and the willingness of the Charity Commissioners to vary the terms. We shall explore shortly the ways in which the Company has sought to rationalise its trusts. Second, the management charges levied by the Company are relatively low. It is true that the level of 'management subsidy' from the corporate income has varied according to the health of the Company's finances, but the charge on the charities has generally stood at around 5-6 per cent of net income. This compares very favourably with most similar trustee bodies.[12]

As an illustration of the limits on the Company's freedom of manoeuvre and the financial constraints imposed by earlier schemes one might consider the fortunes of the almshouses in the immediate post-war years. When the Jones monies were split into separate educational and almshouse charities by the 19th-century reformers, the almshouses at Newland and Monmouth were allocated £1,500 per annum, and the schools the rest. At the time of the split the total income of the charity was about £6,000 per annum, by the late 1950s it was £45,000.[13] The almshouses were not up to modern standards: those at Newland were without light, running water, and indoor sanitation. In 1953 a modernisation programme took place at Newland, which converted them into ten flats brought up to the standard of the Housing Act of 1949. The works cost £6,941: only £941 was available from the repair fund; the rest was met by a £3,000 grant from Gloucester County Council, and a loan from the charity of £3,000, the repayments on which had the effect of reducing the charity's disposable income in the years ahead.[14] At Monmouth, the siting of the almshouses cheek-by-jowl with the School made their relocation highly desirable, but without provision for reallocation between educational and charitable interests the costs were prohibitive. In the event, new almshouses (comprising six double units and 14 singles) were constructed in Monmouth, receiving their residents in December 1961, at a total cost of £43,171 19s. 2d., a large portion of which was borne by a loan from the main charity. It was only with an application to the Charity Commissioners in 1963 to increase the allocation to the almshouses to £4,000 per annum that the finances could be put on an even keel.[15]

The tergiversations of another element of the Jones charity, the Golden Lecture, demonstrate other ways in which the Company has sought to adapt its charities to the needs of a changing society. William Jones had originally provided for a lecturer (that is a preacher who was supposed to supplement the inadequate preaching resources of the Church of England) in the church of St Bartholomew Exchange. The 1871 reform scheme provided for a Lecturer who would give 12 lectures, six in Lent and six in Advent, supplemented by a number of 'Jones Preachers', incumbents serving cures with low incomes within five miles of Haberdashers' Hall.[16] In 1953 the scheme was amended

58 Rev. Basil Watson O.B.E., R.N. (Rtd.), Company Chaplain
(1970-1987), with his churchwarden, Sir Robin Gillett, former Lord
Mayor, at St Lawrence Jewry.

to provide for up to two lecturers each giving at least four lectures (the
preachers continued), but the greater variety did not boost attendance.[17] The
Vicar of St Mary Woolnoth where the lectures were held commented that
attendances were lower than at his other lunch-time services. The Company
responded in 1957 by increasing the number of preachers to up to four in
any one year, and seeking a greater diversity in topics. Lectures should be

59 Rev. Prebendary David Burgess, Company Chaplain (since
1987), before the altar of the church of St Lawrence Jewry.

60   Mrs Susan Howatch (second from left), author and first female
Golden Lecturer in 2001, pictured with the Master, Mr Brian Shawcross,
and Mrs Shawcross.

'of interest to the man in the street'; they should not be 'purely theological';
this would allow lectures to be given by 'eminent divines' on topics such as
communism, divorce, and the colour bar.[18] There does seem to have been an
improvement in the years ahead. Certainly the Company responded indignantly
to a proposal from the Bishop of London in 1969 that a number of trusts
administered by several Companies should be amalgamated to ensure a number
of high quality lectures on the grounds that lectures were poorly attended and
the remuneration inadequate. The Haberdashers claimed their lectures were
well attended, that they had attracted the best preachers, that the rewards
were adequate, and the preachers 'were not in any case attracted by material
considerations'.[19] There were indeed some imaginative programmes. In 1975
the lecturers were asked to take music as their theme. Cliff Richard spoke
on 'Church Music: the Way I see it', Lionel Dakers, Director of the Royal
School of Church Music on 'Church Music and Contemporary Society', and
Dr Allan Wicks, organist at Canterbury Cathedral, on 'Church Music: the
Passionate Art'.[20] That said the number of lectures has progressively shrunk.
Already down to three lectures a year in the 1970s, from 1980 it was agreed
that there should be just one.[21] The Golden Lecture tends to be given by
senior ecclesiastics: in recent years they have included the Rt Rev. and Rt Hon.
David Hope, Archbishop of York (1995), Rt Rev. Michael Baughen, formerly
Bishop of Chester (1996), the Rt Rev. and Rt Hon. Richard Chartres, Bishop
of London (1997), the Rt Rev. Thomas Butler, Bishop of Southwark (1999),
but there has been some variety: in 2000 the lecture was given by the Rt
Hon. Frank Field MP, and in 2001 by the author Susan Howatch, the first
female Golden Lecturer.[22]

The Golden Lecture is only the most prominent of the Company's religious commitments. It has also enjoyed rights of presentation (albeit sometimes shared with others) to 11 livings. The majority were, as we have seen, acquired in the early modern period by the benefactions of Thomas Aldersey and Dame Mary Weld, but the Victorian reorganisation of the Jones charity enabled the acquisition of the patronage of the churches of All Saints and St Catherine (both in Hatcham) and St John the Baptist Hoxton.[23] The shrinkage of the Church of England over the last century has resulted in numerous amalgamations of parishes which has in many cases diluted the Company's patronage. In 1952 the rectory of Awre and chaplaincy of Blakeney were merged to form the united parish of Awre and Blakeney; in 1982 they were further joined with the parish of Newnham, meaning that the right of presentation is now exercised jointly with the Bishop of Gloucester. The Haberdashers continue to take their obligations to the parishes seriously. Individual Liverymen are encouraged to maintain a personal association with particular parishes, and there is an attempt to channel other charitable resources to support the Haberdasher livings where appropriate. The process of rationalisation is inevitable. In 2002 the Company agreed to end the practice of rotating the rights of presentation to the six livings received under the Lady Weld benefaction with Christ's Hospital, and gaining sole rights to three of them (St Peter's with All Saints, Chertsey, All Saints, Wigston Magna, and St Mary Magdalene, Albrighton).[24]

It would be wrong to suggest, however, that the Company is entirely dependent on the legacy of the past. Several new trusts were established over the course of the 20th century. These included prize funds or travelling scholarships (Commander W.C. Northcott, 1959 and P.B. Powell, 1982) or bursaries at the schools (R.T. Hawes, 1968), or further education for pupils of Haberdasher schools (C.R. Picken, 1945, E.T.W. Dodd, 1974).[25] Among the more important donations is that of Thomas Arno (1937) who left the residue of his estate located mostly in Eastbourne, after providing annuities to his family, for broadly defined charitable objects, including the assistance of young men starting in business and the support of pupils at the Company's schools, grants to schools, and donations to hospitals or other causes for the public benefit. Members of the Arno family continue to be closely associated with the Company, and Teddy Elliott (Livery, 1958, Master, 1991), took an interest in the affairs of the Arno charity, and befriended Miss Mary and Mrs Doris Arno.[26] Another general trust was established by trust deed in 1969 on the instructions of Miss Barbara Mabel Pinchin, a non-Haberdasher and friend of Pat Powell, to make grants or loans to poor deserving people, and for other charitable purposes, among which medical charities are prominent. The respective annual incomes of the Arno and Pinchin funds in 1999-2000 were £97,168 and £26,392.[27]

Rather than relying on bequests, there has been an increasing emphasis on the need to channel the charitable giving of company members through the Company. One vehicle has been the St Catherine Foundation established by Dick Liddiard, with the strong encouragement of Brian Jenks in 1970. Members have been encouraged to subscribe, albeit with rather limited success. The charity exists to provide financial assistance to the families of pupils at Haberdasher and other schools and support for other educational purposes. The bursaries are used to enable families struck by unforeseen misfortune, such as death, serious illness and other circumstances affecting the family's ability to meet fees. The Charity aims to continue to support the children affected until the next stage of their education, maintaining an important source of educational and emotional continuity for pupils in what are otherwise very trying circumstances.[28] It has enjoyed mixed success. By the mid-1980s £100,000-£125,000 per annum was being paid by way of grants. In 1985, 77 pupils were benefiting from the fund: they included 21 at the Company's own schools, but recipients were spread through 37 schools and six higher education institutions. By 2000-1 £133,000 was being spent and there were 100 beneficiaries, 15 of them at Haberdasher schools.[29]

Perhaps more successful in attracting the beneficence of members of the Company than the Saint Catherine's Foundation, the capital of which has not grown markedly and remains dependent on annual subventions mostly from the Company's corporate funds, were the fund-raising activities associated with the millennium. A Millennium Committee chaired by Peter Bedford (Livery, 1970, Master, 1995) was formed in 1995, when it was decided to establish an appeal to provide funds equally for the Haberdasher schools and for the Haberdashers' Millennium Treasures Trust.[30] A charitable partnership was established in 1998 (with initial matching contributions of £75,000 apiece) between the Company and Schroders who became the head-lessees of the Garrard House site on its reconstruction in 1998. The aim of the Schroders and Haberdashers' Educational Foundation (S.H.E.F.) is to provide grants for the benefit of the Company's schools and to enhance their facilities. The Treasures Trust was established with the needs of the new Hall in mind to 'acquire, preserve, maintain, and display for the benefit of the public, works of art, artefacts, documents, pictures, carvings, sculptures, and such like material which reflects the historic contribution to, and development of, the life of the City of London by the Haberdashers' Company'.[31] The Millennium Appeal was launched at the Company's dinner at the Mansion House on 5 October 1998, and over the course of the following year the Company hosted a variety of fund-raising events, including a wine-tasting, a race evening, and a concert at the Barbican given by pupils from the Elstree schools. Even so, the appeal did not reach the target figure of £2 million: after a year, only 27 per cent of all Liverymen and Freemen had made a donation, and the fund reached £775,000.[32] It was possible, however, to fund a variety of millennium activities for the schools during millennium year; most notably 90 pupils from the Company's schools were each able to spend two weeks in the Sail Training Association's ship *Stavros Niarchos*. The Schroders and Haberdashers Educational Foundation had made its first grants of £5,600 in 1999, but the volume of support has increased with grants of £10,000 in 2001. The funds have been used to help with objectives as varied as the provision of sound and lighting

61 Royal Hospital and Home Putney: exterior view of new living units.

equipment for drama productions, audio-visual and IT equipment, leadership training programmes, playground markings, and a rowing machine.[33]

As we saw in chapter 2 the Company's effective financial management has transformed the resources available for charitable activity. Some of what used to be called the 'minor charities' (a term now unused in Haberdasher discourse in recognition of their often increased importance) have seen remarkable transformations. As was explained in chapter 2, a small parcel of properties at 289/94 Bishopsgate belonging to the Boddington and Boulter charity and rented at £800 per annum for most of the pre-war period, was sold for £3 million in August 1986 when the area became subject to a redevelopment scheme, thereby significantly boosting the income of the Haberdashers Eleemosynary Charity, into which the Boddington and Boulter assets had been absorbed. The Company's new-found ability to commit its resources to large-scale projects by way of 'pump-priming' was directly related to this income boost.[34]

This increase in funds available in the Haberdashers' Eleemosynary and other charities enabled the Company to undertake a major review of its charitable priorities in 1987, and it was decided to concentrate giving on large grants to a few carefully vetted schemes, provided that the Company could retain an interest in their administration. The first such beneficiaries selected were 'Centrepoint', a charity directed at the homeless young in the capital, the Brain Injury Unit at The Royal Hospital and Home, Putney, and the Royal Surgical Aid Society, which gives support to sufferers from senile dementia and Alzheimer's.[35] The Company's relationship with 'Centrepoint' was particularly fruitful, as it became evident that its involvement acted as a catalyst to other charities to support improved provision in a difficult area of the charity sector.

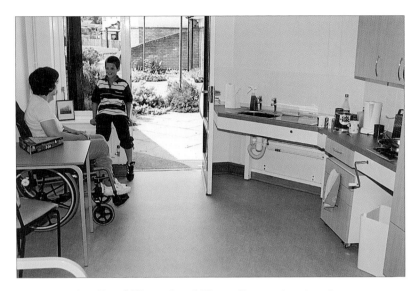

62   Royal Hospital and Home Putney: interior view.

Haberdasher grants financed the purchase, setting up, and initial running costs of a rehabilitation home for ten homeless teenagers in the New Cross area where the Company had long-standing associations. Haberdashers' House, as the hostel was called, was opened in June 1989 by David Scott, Minister for the Disabled. Haberdasher involvement had been initiated by Geoffrey Fox (Livery, 1955, Master, 1986), and was monitored by David Juster (Livery, 1985), who served on the management committee. The Company's support for Haberdashers' House itself ceased from 1995, but they subsequently gave further pump-priming money to other 'Centrepoint' projects, such as £100,000 to a scheme to provide overnight beds in the King's Cross area, and another £100,000 to a housing scheme for seven young people in Hackney. Over the length of its 12-year association with 'Centrepoint', the Company's charities had provided £1.5 million.[36] At the Royal Hospital and Home at Putney (now the Royal Hospital for Neuro-disability), the Company's charities have contributed to the construction of another Haberdashers' House, completed in 1993, a 'transitional living unit' which equips 12 patients at a time with the skills necessary for their return to the community.[37]

Since the late 1980s therefore the Company has been seeking to concentrate its increased charitable activity in targeted areas, but in order to maintain a breadth of concern and a sensitivity to potential new areas of endeavour, from 2001 each Master has been able to select three charities (subject to approval by the Charities Committee), each of which might be supported with grants of up to £10,000 during his year of office. Brian Shawcross, the first such 'patron', selected three local charities in the Gloucester area: a refuge for women and children, a school for children with communication difficulties,

63   H.R.H. Diana Princess of Wales at the opening of Centrepoint's cold
weather shelter in 1997, pictured with the Director, Mr Stephen Hardwicke,
Mr David Juster, Liveryman, and the Master, Mr Teddy Elliott.

and a scheme for placing the homeless unemployed in private homes. This
extends the previous provision by which the Master might select causes for
grants of up to £2,000.[38]

Existing trusts, some of them with quite narrow objectives, have often been
turned to imaginative use. The Jeston trust, for example, concentrates giving
in the Lambeth area, but has been used to support a variety of local projects.
Substantial annual donations have been made from 1999 to 2002 to Hayle's
Charity, one of the Lambeth Endowed Charities, successor to the United
Charities of Lambeth, one of the approved beneficiaries. These donations have
been channelled to small grass-roots local organisations benefiting disadvantaged
people, such as a furniture recycling project and a day centre for homeless
people. To support 'the poor' at St Bartholomew's and St Thomas' Hospitals,
another of the approved objects, substantial support has been given during the
same period to the appropriate medical schools to help relieve the financial
needs of mature fourth-year medical students, often those starting with degrees
in other subjects and with large debts. King Edward's School Witley is the
successor to the Bridewell Hospital Foundation (originally a house of correction
to discipline delinquent youth!), another of the specific beneficiaries, and has
been supported for many years, through bursaries for children from socially
deprived backgrounds.[39] Likewise the Arno monies, directed at young people
starting up in business, have been used to support projects as varied as the
Prince of Wales' Youth Business Trust, the Challenger Trust (giving young
people venture and leadership training), the Hackney Business Venture, and
the Educational Project at Tate Modern. The Pinchin Foundation has funded

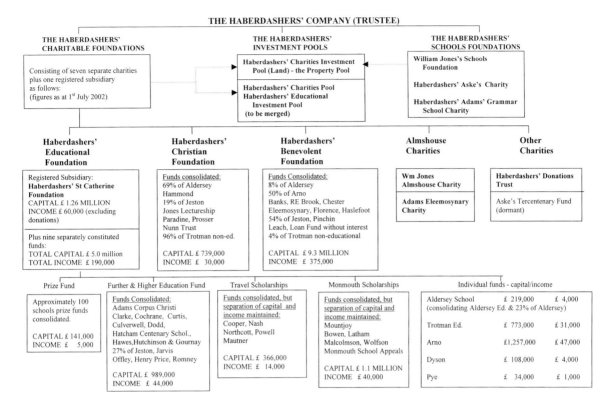

Table 5.1 Structure of the Haberdashers' Company Charities as at 1 July 2002.

convalescent homes, medical research charities and, through the Universal Beneficent Society, help to the needy elderly living within inner-city areas.[40]

The Company has pursued the continuing rationalisation of its charitable activities. In 1992 the Company broached the sensitive subject of the creation of an educational pool, which would reduce management charges and increase investment yields. Although it was always recognised that there was no possibility of taking action detrimental to the principal objects of a charity, it might be possible for wealthier charities to make loans to poorer ones, and surplus funds might potentially be applied elsewhere under the cy-près doctrine. A lot of work was put into a scheme, particularly by Owen Swingland, but it did not find favour with the Charity Commissioners, and it was recognised that it was a matter of great sensitivity with the schools, particularly Monmouth, who might perceive that they were losers. The idea was eventually dropped.[41]

The abortive Haberdashers' Foundation proposals of 1992-4 illustrate some of the constraints under which the Company operates in pursuing rationalisation. But elsewhere it has been more successful, aided by a more sympathetic and increasingly flexible Charity Commission. In 1978 several of the smaller trusts were incorporated into the Haberdashers' Eleemosynary Charity, the terms of which offered greater flexibility in their distribution. The object of the fund was defined as grants to poor people in hardship or distress, not more than two-thirds of which should go to freemen of the Company of the city, their wives, and children.[42] This still left over a hundred trusts and prize funds and the most important step in the direction of rationalisation was the consolidation in 2002 of the remaining trusts into three new registered charities with broadly defined objectives. They are the Haberdashers' Benevolent Foundation concerned primarily with welfare, the Haberdashers' Educational Foundation which brings together various educational funds (though excluding the Jones, Aske and Adams Grammar School charities), and the Haberdashers' Christian Foundation which will be used primarily to support the Company's livings, the Jones' preachers, and the Jones Lecturer. This has been a complex and delicate undertaking, as an important objective was to produce a scheme which as far as possible reflected the donors' original wishes, and in which their identity could be retained. The resulting structure together with an indication of the approximate income of each of the trusts in 2002 is indicated in table 5.1.[43]

Something of the transformation in the Company's charitable giving is clear from the table (5.2) below. Even taking into account the fact that the figures for 2002 include £224,000 of the Millennium Fund proceeds the figures are impressive, given the fact that the retail price index approximately doubled over the period 1985-2002. Once expressed in 1999 prices, the figures demonstrate the huge increases in resources available in real terms from the 'other charities', that is the traditionally smaller funds (like Boddington and Boulter) now boosted by wise investment decisions.[44]

In the year to June 2002, the Charities Committee made over 400 grants to individuals totalling £286,000, and there were over 250 donations to charities totalling over £1 million. These figures of course exclude the £2.5 million paid to the schools from their own trusts (Adams, Jones, and Aske). The prominence of education in the Haberdashers' charitable activity is clear from the fact that it accounted for 53.6 per cent of grants in 2001-2; 24.6 per cent went to disadvantaged people, 4 per cent to the Church, 4.3 per cent to young people, 5.1 per cent to health, and 8.3 per cent to arts and sport.

The developments we have been looking at have been assisted by changes in the legal framework within which the charities are managed. Some of the changes such as the Statements of Recommended Accounting Practice (S.O.R.P.s) of 1995 and 2000 have resulted in greater transparency. The policy of consolidation and rationalisation has been assisted by changes in the attitude of the Charity Commission which during the 1990s began seeing itself as an adviser and facilitator as much as a regulator and controller. The Company has seen the benefit of this through the greater flexibility provided in new Schemes. For example, the Jones's Almshouse Charity Scheme sealed in 2001 allowed the Company and the local committees far more discretion in the management of the Monmouth and Newland almshouses than previously. The Charities Acts of 1992 and 1993 gave trustees the power to wind up small charities and to

Table 5.2 Haberdashers' Grant Making and Almshouse Charities/Trusts
(excluding schools foundations)
Figures in brackets represent values at 1999 prices.

	1985 (£000s)		2002 (£000s)	
1. INCOME				
Haberdashers St Catherine Foundation	98	(171)	170	(160)
William Jones Almshouse Charity	38	(66)	59	(55)
Other Charities/Trusts	256	(447)	834	(782)
Total income	392	(684)	1063	(997)
2. EXPENDITURE				
Haberdashers' St Catherine Foundation	120	(209)	126	(118)
William Jones's Almshouse Charity	37	(66)	61	(57)
Other Charities/Trusts (including accumulated income)	248	(432)	1331	(1248)
Total expenditure	405	(707)	1518	(1423)
Breakdown of other Charities/Trusts Expenditure				
Company Poor	15	(26)	16	(15)
Scholarships and Exhibitions	23	(40)	175	(164)
Other	210	(366)	1140	(1069)
Total (other charities/trusts)	248	(432)	1331	(1248)
3. INVESTED CAPITAL				
Haberdashers' St Catherine Foundation	321	(560)	1258	(1180)
William Jones's Almshouse Charity	27	(47)	309	(290)
Other Charities/Trusts	2535	(4423)	16535	(15510)
Total endowment	2883	(5030)	18102	(16980)

spend or transfer the capital to other charities, which has proved useful in the consolidation exercise. The Trustee Act 2000 replaced the earlier Trustee Investment Act 1961, removing many of the previous constraints on investment powers of trustees. This has been of practical help in the management of the Company's charitable investments.[45]

There is a danger in pursuing rationalisation that the personal element of charitable provision is lost. It is true that there has been some reorientation of activity away from the Company's 'own people'. The widows of Liverymen are no longer as prominent in the discussions of the Charities Committee as they were in the 1940s, but the Company continues to take a keen interest in former members of staff, and its Almoners (often recruited from retired members of the school staff) undertake a great deal of personal visiting of elderly people with which the Company has a connection, and providing invaluable support to otherwise very lonely people. The Almoners' work for the Clerk, who reports significant matters to the Charities Committee. The Company also continues to offer support to individual pupils at its schools, not only through the St Catherine's bursaries but also through grants for gap-year activities. It should also be emphasised that in choosing new charities to support, the Company looks for causes where individual Company members are already closely involved, and efforts are made to bring representatives of the charities to events at the Hall, by way of enhancing the dialogue between the charities and the Company's members.[46]

There has been some debate within the Company over the past 25 years about the proper areas within which charitable resources should be concentrated. In 1992, for example, Christopher Bostock and Geoffrey Fox initiated a discussion as to whether more of the Company's resources should not be directed towards the educational sector. They argued that in view of the primacy of the Haberdashers among livery companies in the field of education, this is the area in which more should be done. It needs to be recognised, as did the sponsors of the 1992 debate, that some dispersal of charitable endeavour is inevitable given the terms of the charitable trusts the Company administers, but there is no doubting the centrality of the Company's educational mission, and this will be more fully treated in the next chapter.[47]

Chapter Six

The Company's Schools

The Haberdashers have come to make a virtue of the varied character of their schools. It is a variety which owes a lot to the different financial circumstances of the trusts under which they are administered combined with the impact of changing government policy. Because of their varied resources and catchment areas the Haberdasher schools emerged very differently from the 1944 Education Act. At Monmouth, the girls' and boys' schools successfully applied for direct grant status, becoming fee-paying schools on condition that 25 per cent of their annual entry was offered to the Local Education Authority as free places. The West Monmouthshire School, which the Company had regarded with some disfavour because of the drain it posed on resources the Haberdashers felt should be applied to Monmouth, was handed over to the County in 1955, in return for a revision of the 1910 scheme in favour of the Monmouth schools.[1] The fate of the Aske schools was more varied. The trustees applied for direct grant status for Acton and Hampstead, but because the income of the charity was insufficient to support four schools, it was decided that the Hatcham schools should enjoy voluntary controlled status, whereby the L.C.C. undertook responsibility for all maintenance and tuition, although the Company retained the freehold of all the school properties.[2] The resources of the Adams charity, supported by rural properties, never matched those of Aske and Jones, so yet another route was taken by the Newport school. In 1949 the school was granted voluntary-aided status by which the Governors retained responsibility for maintenance and the provision of new buildings subject to grants from the Ministry of Education of 50 per cent towards costs incurred in external repairs and improvements. Newport provided a free education, but its special feature, of which much would be made when it faced hostile local authorities, was that it provided boarding within the state sector.[3] Bunbury also went for voluntary-aided status, but under pressure from the Vicar, Canon Maurice Ridgway, it was declared in 1956 to be a Church of England school, raising the possibility of tapping diocesan funds for building works albeit at the price of inserting another partner in the decision-making process. However, the opening of Tarporley Secondary Modern in 1958 and the closure of the local girls' school in 1960 necessitated changes at Bunbury if it was to remain viable. It was transformed from a public elementary school educating children between seven and 14 to a mixed primary school teaching children aged five to eleven.[4]

The difference in school status had major implications for the governance of the several schools, and therefore the control the Company could exercise over them. This is best illustrated by comparing the composition of the post-

64 Past Master, Mr David Sime, leading the dancing around the maypole at Bunbury, 1990.

war governing bodies at Hampstead and Acton with that at Hatcham. At the direct grant North London schools the Haberdashers dominated the schools' governing body, appointing nine of the 19 Governors; of the others one was appointed by the Lord Mayor and Aldermen, one by the Common Council, two by the London County Council, four by the County of Middlesex, one by the Senate of the University of London, and one by Acton Borough Council. But at Hatcham (voluntary controlled) the Company appointed only one third of the Governors. Voluntary-aided as opposed to voluntary-controlled status made a great difference, for at Newport the ten Foundation Governors comprised the Master of the Company, seven appointed by the Company, and two by the Old Boys' Association, easily counterbalancing the five Representative Governors appointed by the L.E.A. These differences were, as we shall see, to be of great significance in determining the varying futures of the schools in the face of the schemes of successive governments for the reorganisation of education.[5]

In common with all schools, those of the Haberdashers have had to respond to the need for improved and expanded facilities, reflecting the increasing stress on scientific subjects, the desirability of better facilities for sport, music, and drama, and more recently the growing prominence in the curriculum of both Craft, Design, and Technology, and I.T. Here is not the place to chronicle the building programmes at the different schools, but it is important to recognise their significance in relations between the schools and the Company, and between the Company and the State. The voluntary-aided schools in particular have sometimes had a difficult time in raising the necessary funds for building

65   Bunbury Church of England Primary School, new wing completed in 1993.

projects. The need for additional classrooms at Bunbury, where children were being taught in the Victorian school room of 1874, had been recognised in 1939, but the new classrooms were not provided until 1962-3. Costs escalated from an estimated £750 in 1939 to over £20,000 by the time the buildings were provided.[6] At Newport the need for increased boarding accommodation was met by the purchase of Aston Hall (1948), Beaumaris House (1949), and Roddam House (1953), but all required delicate negotiations with Shropshire County Council and the Ministry of Education to secure the necessary approvals. But other necessary projects were delayed. The gymnasium, promised twenty years previously, only opened in 1957, financed by the sale of the Cadbury milk processing works, part of the Knighton estate. The building of a new science block and Masters' Common Room in 1960 was financed by the sale of the rest of the Knighton estate, but the charity's slender resources retarded other necessary works in succeeding years. The Governors remained alert to opportunities. In 1967 they used the sale of Aston Hall and the Wellington Road playing fields to purchase Longford Hall for £40,000 giving additional boarding accommodation and a new site for the playing fields.[7] It was to prove a wise investment, for the sale in 2001 (after years of hard work by Tim Jackson-Stops (Livery, 1964), formerly an Assistant, to secure the necessary planning consents) of a small area of surplus land at Longford Hall for property development for £1 million (valued five years before that at just £10,000) has provided a ring-fenced fund intended for support of the school's many listed buildings.[8]

Even where the resources of the charity were more ample, as at Monmouth, building works often had the potential to sour relations between the Company

66 H.R.H. The Princess Margaret accompanied by the Master, Mr Teddy Elliott, led by Miss Helen Gichard, Headmistress, and followed by Mr Michael Clarke, Chairman of Governors, at the opening of the swimming pool at Monmouth Girls' School, 1992.

67 Monmouth Boys' School: the Sports Complex, opened in 1998, at night.

and the schools. Major disagreements emerged in the mid-1950s with Cecil Cullingford, the Headmaster of Monmouth School, who was convinced that the Governors' plans sited new buildings too close to the swimming bath. The conflict had its comic element. Cullingford, who believed in pursuing 'the hard right rather than the easier wrong', took to a Governors' meeting a highly amplified and orchestrated tape-recording of the noise coming from the baths.[9] Behind the row probably lay poor communications between the School, the Company, and the Governors; interestingly, Cullingford's resignation in 1956 did not immediately improve matters for in 1958 the Haberdashers were complaining about a lack of clarity in the Governors' requests, as they shifted their ground on the priority to be given to the new science block as opposed to other facilities, which the Court seems to have thought more pressing. Commander Prevett, the Clerk, wrote a blistering letter to the Clerk to the Monmouth Governors which makes it clear how far things had broken down. He denied that the Company was interfering with the Governors' role, but emphasised its responsibilities as trustee. Cullingford's replacement as Headmaster, J.R.M. Senior, was accused of having extravagant plans for the science laboratories, which First Warden P.C. Bull (Livery, 1916, Master, 1958), an experienced Chemistry lecturer at Imperial College, considered impractical. The Haberdashers' more modest plans for science accommodation could be combined with additional classrooms. Although the Company had backed the Headmaster, the Minister of Education had confirmed their reservations ('such a letter cannot and will not be ignored by the trustees', Prevett added menacingly). 'The Company feels it has erred in agreeing to an extravagant scheme to placate a new Head in the face of the Headmasters' Conference and Archbishop of Canterbury's criticism.' Monmouth was in a bad way, having been taken off the list of H.M.C. schools, and it took R.F. Glover's Headship from 1959 to restore academic standards and good working relations with the Company.[10]

The Company's concern to maintain the capital of the trusts supporting the schools sometimes results in an understandable tension with school Governors anxious to press ahead with immediate building projects. The introduction in 1980 of the 'Bostock Rules' for the repayment of loans to the schools, discussed in chapter 2, may have been painful and occasioned some tension with the Monmouth Governors, who had just embarked on the building of a new Science Block, but the new rules were designed to bring an air of reality into the management of resources.[11]

The major determinant of the fortunes of the so-called 'North London' schools was the decision to move to Elstree. The Boys' School at Hampstead was especially poorly located. It was surrounded by housing estates which sent few pupils to the school; boys commuted in from the north through rush-hour traffic; the playing fields were distant, and the school site highly restricted. It had been decided in principle in 1954 that the school should move when the opportunity arose, but a suitable site was not found until 1958, when Lord Aldenham offered part of his Elstree estate, occupied since 1941 by the B.B.C.[12]

68 Elstree Girls' School: The Art Department.

69 Haberdashers' Monmouth School for Girls: The Hamersley Music Centre, opened in 1999.

It was a bold move and one which seriously strained the charity's resources. The Company successfully pushed the L.C.C. to increase its offer price for the Hampstead School site (with the playing fields, Chase Lodge, and the preparatory school at Flower Lane) to £244,000, but the cost of the new school escalated from an original estimate of £250,000 to a final price of £459,042 12s.1d. Part of the gap was closed by an appeal which raised about £30,000, but that still left a sizeable amount to be met by loans.[13] Moreover, the tight budget meant that the facilities were never adequate, and the vulnerability of the Aske charity finances meant that the Governors had to apply to the Ministry for a sharp increase in fees in 1963.[14] Nevertheless, the decision to move was undoubtedly correct for the standards and reputation of the school soared. Although money was tight, the Governors, mindful from the Hampstead years of the dangers of a restrictive site, purchased an additional 44 acres from Lord Aldenham in 1963.[15] In subsequent years key building projects such as the Technology Block (opened by the Rt Hon. Margaret Thatcher as Secretary of State for Education in 1971), the Arts Teaching Block (1970), and the Music School (1973) were assisted by a series of remarkable donations from an anonymous benefactor.[16]

As the boys settled into the new premises at Elstree in the early 1960s it had been determined that the girls would not move for another fifteen years at least,[17] but by 1970 the pressing need for the modernisation of facilities at Acton and the local Council's reluctance to continue funding the free places provided for by direct grant made the matter urgent. Some other sites such as Ruislip and Ickenham were considered at the instigation of Miss Gillett, Headmistress at Acton, who did not necessarily share the Court's enthusiasm for a move in proximity to the Boys' School. The Company, however, was convinced that a move to Elstree would be for the best.[18] The negotiations proved difficult, with Ealing Borough Council blowing hot and cold over the purchase of the Acton site (agreement was eventually reached in 1972) and Watford Rural District Council opposing the infringement of green belt building restrictions at Elstree.[19] This decision was overruled by Hertfordshire County Council, but further problems ensued with the building as costs escalated. The architect had estimated £900,000 in April 1972; by the time the foundation stone was laid in November 1972 that had risen to £1.172 million, and a year later costs were at £1.276 million.[20]

By the early 1960s the limitations of the Butler Act had become apparent as secondary education still remained class bound, and the Labour Party came to see the solution in replacing grammar schools with comprehensives and in attacking fee-paying schools.[21] As Commander Prevett, the Haberdashers' Clerk, wrote in 1961, 'we know the views of the Socialist Party [sic] on public schools (including direct grant)… it is probable that within thirty years these schools will be nationalised, in which case their endowments will be seized by the state'.[22] The Company explored the possibilities of protecting its educational trusts against nationalisation by varying their purpose, but reluctantly concluded that such a course would be opposed by the Minister of Education, the Charity Commissioners, and the local authorities: nothing could be done.[23] Ian Bowater pressed repeatedly from 1963 for the well endowed Monmouth schools to go fully independent, but his was not a majority view.[24] In the event, when Labour came to power in 1964, the full-blown attack on fee-paying schools did not materialise, but a push towards comprehensive education was made. Schemes of reorganisation on comprehensive principles had already been introduced under the Conservatives (there were 300 comprehensives in 1964), and Tony Crosland's (Secretary of State for Education from 1965) Circular 10/65 put its weight behind comprehensives by calling on local authorities to submit plans for comprehensive schooling, although without the compulsion of statute. By 1970, when the Conservatives returned to power, there were 1,000 comprehensives (educating 30 per cent of pupils in secondary education), but the policy continued under the Heath government which left the organisation of secondary education to the discretion of local authorities: by 1974 there were 2,000 comprehensives with 60 per cent of secondary pupils. The status of direct grant schools (there were 178 nationally in 1970 accommodating 3 per cent of the school population and 10 per cent of sixth formers) had been left ambiguous in circular 10/65; they were supposed to 'associate' with schemes of comprehensive reorganisation, but, as one educational commentator of the time remarked, this was rather 'like asking the Athenaeum to consider ways in which it could become a Youth Centre'.[25] Labour's more radical intentions were apparent in the Donnison Report published in the spring of 1970 which recommended the abolition of direct grant. This was shelved by the Conservatives, but the proposal was part of Labour's manifesto commitment when it returned to power in 1974. Reg Prentice as Secretary of State announced in 1975 that direct grant would be

70   Elstree Boys' School: The Library, opened in 1992.

phased out from September 1976, leaving the Monmouth and Elstree schools with the option of either going independent or being absorbed into the state system. Labour did not, however, implement its threat to withdraw charitable status from the private schools.[26]

The Company had therefore been able to prepare for the loss of direct grant for some time. A report in 1969 on the implications of the withdrawal of direct grant had suggested that the Elstree Boys' School would remain viable, the Girls' at Acton only just.[27] The Aske Board of Governors resolved in October 1970 that should the Donnison Report be implemented the schools would go independent, but it is striking that some prominent members of the Court including Sir Robin Brook and Sir Richard Jenks were opposed on the grounds of the issue of trust (should an institution founded for poor boys go fully 'private'?): Jenks requested that it be a matter of record that he was 'opposed to independent status for the Aske schools in any circumstances' (it is a matter of some irony that thirty years later his son Brian was to be Chairman of Governors of the now fully independent Elstree schools!).[28] By the time the blow fell in 1975 the Acton Girls' School had joined the Boys' at Elstree, positioning it better to face the challenges of fully independent status. At Monmouth the prognosis for an independent Girls' School had not been good in 1969, though the Boys' was seen as viable without direct grant. A review by management consultants in 1973 was more sanguine, as there had been an increase in the numbers of professionals on new estates: both schools, it was concluded, would remain viable so long as boarding was increased.[29] When Reg Prentice announced the phasing out of direct grant from 1976 it was decided that all four schools should go independent.[30]

The Hatcham schools had escaped serious pressure to go comprehensive in the later 1960s because the I.L.E.A. was Conservative-controlled from 1967 to 1970, and the comprehensive schemes in the London area had only involved secondary moderns and existing comprehensives; the grammar schools were left untouched.[31] But when Labour took control of the I.L.E.A. in 1970, the climate changed. A scheme was drawn up in 1972 by which a co-educational lower school for 11 to 14-year-olds would operate in one of the existing sets of school buildings, while the sale of the other school site would fund the building of new twin boys' and girls' upper schools (14 plus) and a mixed sixth form on part of the playing fields. But the proposal foundered on Secretary of State Margaret Thatcher's hostility to the segregation of 11 to 14-year-olds.[32] With Labour in power again after 1974 the pressure mounted once more, and in 1975 the I.L.E.A. announced that selection would have to end by September 1977. The negotiations were skilfully handled by Sir Maurice Bathurst Q.C. (Livery, 1964, Master, 1980), himself an old Askean, as Chairman of Governors. Initially the I.L.E.A. had proposed to merge the Boys' and Girls' Schools each with another local school, which would have threatened the schools' identities and their voluntary-controlled status. The deal which was eventually negotiated with the I.L.E.A. in 1976 adopted a comprehensive system at the Hatcham schools but preserved their voluntary-controlled status and scotched the merger proposals. Comprehensive reorganisation at Hatcham also brought about some modest but much needed expenditure on buildings (including a new sixth form block at the Boys' School and facilities for art and craft, music practice, drama, as well as a staff room at the Girls' School). The most important feature of the arrangements which eased the transition was the agreement on admissions with the I.L.E.A. negotiated by Bathurst. Control over admissions would remain in the control of the school heads subject to recruitment of 25 per cent from the upper ability bands, 50 per cent from the middle, and 25 per cent from the lower. Moreover, the Schools' catchment area was to be broader than normal: while recruiting mainly from the Boroughs of Lewisham, Greenwich, and Southwark, they continued to admit up to ten children a year from other boroughs. This undoubtedly made the transition from grammar school to comprehensive an easier one.[33]

The survival of the Adams School at Newport was still more vulnerable to comprehensive reorganisation. The viability of comprehensives required four-form entry in order that they could offer the full range of courses; the existing stock of schools in Newport comprised the two-form entry Adams School, the one-form entry girls grammar school, and the secondary modern school at Burton Borough. The L.E.A.'s proposals for a comprehensive school at Burton Borough were accompanied by the suggestion that the catchment area for Adams should be expanded and the number of pupils from Newport reduced, but this encountered a storm of local opposition, and the plan was shelved in 1971. Successive plans to merge the two grammar schools foundered because of the lack of funds for the building work at Adams necessary to bring it about. Throughout the negotiations, the Haberdashers backed the

71 H.R.H. The Princess Margaret and Dr Elizabeth Sidwell, Headmistress, at the opening of the Bostock Building, Aske's College, Hatcham, 17 November 1993.

Governors in their desire to retain voluntary-aided status and to maintain the distinctive character of the school as a state boarding establishment.[34] A new scheme was put forward in 1972-3 for a three-form co-educational grammar school with a significant boarding element but, although approved by Margaret Thatcher in February 1974, it collapsed with the change of government later in the month.[35] The Education Act of 1976, which compelled L.E.A.s to implement universal comprehensive education, signalled the opening of a new round of local conflict. The Haberdashers seriously considered independence, commissioning the Whitehead Report which made it clear that this was not a viable option; in any case plans for independence were scuppered by the L.E.A.'s insistence on compensation for the loss of free school places that would ensue. For the Newport area the L.E.A. put forward proposals for two 11-18 comprehensive co-educational schools both with sixth forms, but the scheme would have involved significant building works which the charity could not afford, therefore threatening the voluntary-aided status of the school. The Tory-controlled L.E.A. remained committed to the scheme after the General Election of May 1979, but its proposals were rejected by the Secretary of State for Education, Mark Carlisle, in August 1980 on the grounds that this was not the best use of resources.[36]

Although Adams had survived the threat of comprehensive reorganisation its viability was threatened by falling school rolls, the decline in boarding, and the increasing disrepair of its buildings. There was little that the Company could do, given the limits of the charity's resources which were not properly understood in the local community. David Taylor, then Headmaster of Adams, records that the Company's sympathy 'reminded me of the sympathy accorded to the

72   Adams Grammar School: Sixth Form students in the Taylor Building.

terminally ill'.[37] At the end of 1985 the County Council put forward proposals for the closure of Adams, concentrating pupils on Burton Borough, and moving the sixth formers to the New College at Wellington. The Governors, backed by the Haberdashers, were able to exploit the ensuing local protests (mainly it has to be admitted about the loss of a local sixth form rather than the loss of the grammar school) and the government's sympathy for grammar schools, to ensure that the L.E.A.'s proposals were rejected by Kenneth Baker in December 1987.[38] Conservative sympathy for diversity of educational provision proved to be the school's salvation, for the Educational Reform Act of 1988 offered the possibility of escaping L.E.A. control through the adoption of Grant Maintained status, by which the school would receive its funding for money direct from central government. There would no longer be political appointees among the Governors, but they would be replaced by five elected parent Governors. Grant Maintained status was energetically pursued by the Governors with the full support of the Haberdashers, but in the teeth of the County Council's opposition. The parents voted 557:54 in favour of the proposals and by September 1990 Adams Grammar School was incorporated as a Grant Maintained school.[39] It was not of course the immediate panacea to the school's ills, for there were soon disappointments over the school's bid for capital funding because of tight government spending constraints. Nevertheless in March 1992 the school was allocated £500,000 under the Technology Schools Initiative which enabled the first serious building work at the school in over twenty years.[40]

The significance of the Thatcher years for the Haberdasher state schools should not be underestimated, for the Company's rhetoric of 'distinctive character' echoed ministerial priorities about educational pluralism and competition. The introduction of the Assisted Places scheme in 1980 provided a subsidy for able pupils from poorer backgrounds to move from the state to the private sector, though whether it met the aims of its promoters in benefiting the able working-class child or favoured middle-class families with cash-flow problems, is a moot point! The scheme was enthusiastically embraced by most of the former direct grant schools.[41] The early years of the Thatcher government had seen more radical plans for educational reform founder on the rocks of opposition from the teaching profession, but a more radical departure was represented by Kenneth Baker's Education Reform Act of 1988.[42] At Adams, the Act ensured the survival of the grammar school and gave the Company enhanced influence within the governing body. At Hatcham it offered opportunities of a different kind for the schools were converted into a City Technology College (C.T.C.). The Conservative government's intention in promoting C.T.C.s was to provide children from a wide ability range with a technologically enriched learning environment in schools which would become 'beacons of excellence' funded by partnership between the taxpayer and private sponsors. The C.T.C. project nationally cannot really be counted a success because the new schools attracted minimal interest from businesses (who after all were paying large amounts in corporate taxation and in many cases already engaged in partnerships with schools in the state sector) leaving the Treasury to pick up the bulk of the costs.[43] From the Haberdashers' point of view, however, it was a golden opportunity: the advantages of C.T.C. status lay in the Company's association with the cutting edge of educational innovation, the enhancement of two of its Schools by the injection of substantial funds from central government, and the recovery of greater control from the local authority. The funding agreement entered into by the Company with the D.E.S. on 21 December 1990 provided that the Haberdashers would lease on a pepper-corn rent the site of the Schools valued in 1990 at £3.445 million to a specially constituted C.T.C. Trust and provide £1 million from Aske's Charity towards costs over the first five years of the Schools' operation as C.T.C.s, while the Exchequer would furnish £5.5 million. The reconstituted Governing Body of the C.T.C. consisted of three persons appointed by the Haberdashers' Company, one by the Secretary of State, up to seven other nominees of the Company and this group co-opted four parents, the two heads, two teacher representatives, and two representatives of the local community. The College opened in September 1991 as a C.T.C. with single-sex education in the schools up to the age of 16 and a co-educational sixth form.[44]

Needless to say the C.T.C. project was only implemented in the face of tenacious opposition from the I.L.E.A. in its expiring days, and opinion within the Schools and the local community was divided. However, the opposition was beaten off in large part due to the tenacity with which the cause was pursued by the Chairman of Governors, Christopher Bostock. The main arguments deployed against the Haberdashers' scheme (with varying degrees of emphasis) centred on doubts about a potentially restricted curriculum, the apparent failure of additional private sponsorship and the consequent concentration of large sums of taxpayers' money on a limited number of children, the sense that the Schools were already functioning as 'beacons of excellence', hostility to the merging of the Boys' and Girls' Schools (as the government had refused to sanction separate C.T.C.s for the Boys' and Girls' Schools; a majority of the parents and teachers at the Girls' School had initially opposed the scheme), and the problem of assurances to existing staff about the security of their posts. Almost as much controversy was aroused over the methods used to fight the campaign as over the original proposals themselves. When the proposal first came before the Governing Body in April 1988 the I.L.E.A. instructed the four teacher representatives that they could not vote as they had a pecuniary interest in the outcome, an action which was subsequently upheld in the High Court. The issue was heavily politicised with the eight Labour appointees consistently voting against the scheme, while the other nine Governors (two non-Labour appointees, two parents, and the five Foundation Governors) supported it. The next flashpoint occurred over the consultation process concerning the fate of the Schools, begun in May 1988 and lasting six months. The I.L.E.A. claimed that the period should have been longer, but ultimately lost its case at the High Court and in the Court of Appeal. Meanwhile it sought to ensure that the two non-Labour Governors voted in accordance with the Authority's policy and, when they refused to do so, removed them from office three days before the Governors were due to meet and take a decision on 20 January 1989. This action was contested by the two Governors concerned whose case the Haberdashers took to the High Court and were successful in the Court of Appeal and in the House of Lords. The Board of Governors took their decision in favour of the C.T.C. option which was followed by a favourable ballot of parents in May 1989. However, in spite of the support given by the Governing Body, parents, and teachers, the I.L.E.A. nevertheless continued its efforts to manipulate the composition of the Governing Body by attempting to remove a Parent Governor whose child was to leave the school in July 1989 although there was a clear understanding that the appointment should be for the whole school year. Again the I.L.E.A. was taken to Court, this time settling at the door of the Court and agreeing to reinstate the parent and pay her costs. Yet another tactic was the instruction from the I.L.E.A. that the Governing Body should split into two in the hope that a vote against the C.T.C. project might be won on the Governing Body of the Girls' School where opposition had always been stronger. The application was turned down by the Secretary of State, and the I.L.E.A. lost further cases in the High Court and Court of Appeal in its efforts to overturn his verdict. Next the I.L.E.A., acting jointly with Lewisham Borough Council, contested the Secretary of State's closure notice, losing yet more legal battles in the High Court and Court of Appeal in February and May 1990. The sorry tale is an indication of the ferocious politicisation of educational issues wrought by the Education Reform Act.[45]

The emergence of 'New Labour', however, was accompanied by a higher level of consensus on educational policy between the parties than had been the case in the bitterly contested ground of the 1970s and 1980s. Labour abandoned its plans to impose V.A.T. on private school fees and to remove the tax breaks gained through charitable status; it embraced diversity, recognising that schools specialising in music and technology could select according to aptitude in these areas. The Haberdashers had entertained David Blunkett (then Shadow Education Minister) to lunch in July 1996 and he had expressed himself impressed by the diversity of the Company's schools.[46] The election of the Blair government in 1997 did not involve the kind of disruption to educational policy that previous changes of regime had entailed. It is true that the abolition of Grant Maintained status meant that Adams reverted to Voluntary Aided status in September 1999, but its future is now much more secure, with Technology College status as a specialist school giving increased emphasis to mathematics, science, and technology, pupil numbers at a record high (775 in 2001), and a very successful appeal supplemented by a large government grant providing money for a new Sports Hall and conversion of the gymnasium to a new Arts and Drama Centre.[47]

The Government's decision to abolish the Assisted Places scheme (to fund the reduction of primary school class sizes) has been met by providing bursaries from funds set aside out of endowment income, and parents in difficulties can turn to the St Catherine's Foundation.[48] New Labour has so far proved to be far less hostile to independent schools than its predecessors, and the Company has taken an interest in the new stress on the private sector co-operating with state schools. In 2001 Sir Peter Lampl, a philanthropist who has identified greater state/private co-operation as a key objective, was guest of honour and principal speaker at a Livery Dinner.[49]

Discussion of the changing constitutional position of the schools and its relationship to political change runs the risk of obscuring the degree to which the Company's relationship with its schools has intensified in the later 20th century. Looking back to the 1950s, deputations were occasions of extended sociability rather than an exploration of areas of mutual concern. Today's senior members of the Company, asked about the deputations of the 1950s, recall hampers of wine being brought down from the Company's cellars and lengthy luncheons followed by games of bridge. Some of the 'old guard' had some pretty reactionary views on education: Ned Goddard, the Headmaster of Hatcham Boys, recalled that he was informed that 'what was needed to produce a good school was to make every boy join the Corps and not be afraid to use the cane'. We have seen how at Monmouth in the 1950s there had been difficulties of communication between the Company and the schools. The image, however, sometimes belied a more hard-headed reality. The sugar-magnate Dick Liddiard, as Chairman of the Elstree Governors, may have turned up in his chauffeur-driven Rolls Royce puffing on his cigar, the epitome of the old City, but he is remembered in the schools as constantly fertile in ideas and responsible for much financial innovation.[50] Indeed, by the 1980s, things were generally more professional. In 1985 it was noted that the reporting back to the Court was inconsistent, and it was therefore agreed that each deputation should seek to assess the effectiveness of the Head, Bursar, the morale of staff

73   The Monmouth Deputation, led by the Master, Mr Bruce Sturgess, setting out from the *King's Head* in 1994.

and pupils and their general appearance, the maintenance of buildings, the conditions of formal teaching and private study, and the state of boarding accommodation. It was also agreed that presentations should be made by the Head or senior members of staff to provide insights for those who had not recently visited. Contact between staff and pupils and the members of the deputation was to be encouraged.[51] It is important to realise that deputations foster two-way communication flows: as P.B. Powell observed in 1980 'the relationship between the Governors and the Heads was of a nature which was best fostered by persuasion and informal talks rather than by issuing directives'.[52] Indeed, by the mid-1990s it was recognised that there was a danger of deputations having the quality of inspections, and potentially blurring the lines of responsibility between the Company as trustee and that of the school Governors whose responsibility school standards properly are. Therefore in July 1999 it was agreed that deputations should endeavour to make the Company better informed about all elements of the school community and that they should involve the wider Haberdasher community: Freemen, Heads, Heads of department and senior management from other schools, the Company's professional advisers, and the S.H.E.F. trustees were all encouraged to attend.[53] This represents a continuation and intensification of efforts to involve Company members more fully in the life of the schools. Mindful that the Livery is a seedbed for school Governors, there has been a drive to involve them more fully in deputations. Whereas no Liverymen had attended deputations in 1983, four years later the Clerk noted with satisfaction that the number attending was 27; by 2000 no fewer than 100 people (admittedly a number swollen by representatives from the Company's professional advisers and other schools) had attended a deputation that year. Liverymen have also been encouraged, perhaps with varying degrees of success, to give talks and lectures at the schools. The newsletters have become gradually more informative about the schools, and Company receptions are regularly used as conduits of news of developments at the schools.[54]

The Company has sought in a variety of ways to foster discussion among the schools of issues of common concern. In 1985 the first of a number of Schools Symposia was held with representatives from industry, the universities, and other schools. In October 1993, at a time of considerable anxiety about the implications of the new testing regime, representatives of 34 schools associated with Livery Companies attended another symposium in the presence of Eric Forth, then Schools Minister. Further conferences were held in 1997 and 2001, while in 2002 the Governors of all the schools were encouraged to attend a joint conference.[55] In 1992 the Company appointed Martin Marriott, the former Headmaster of Canford School, as its first Educational Adviser. His role was to provide independent and pragmatic advice to the management teams at the schools and to alert the Haberdashers' Education Committee to the implications of changes in the educational world. His four years in that role have been followed by other well respected, recently retired Heads.[56]

The Company has also actively sought to promote knowledge of its role among staff and pupils at all the schools. In the years after the war the Company must have appeared rather distant. There were occasional visits from pupils as during the Company's 500th anniversary celebrations in 1948, the laying of the foundation stone and opening of the post-war hall; pupils from the London schools regularly provided choirs and entertainment at publication lunches; members occasionally attended school carol services and plays.[57] There were sceptical voices; in 1965 the Revd Anthony Cope expressed his doubts about a St Paul's service for the Aske schools, since he thought it quite wrong for the pupils to attend church 'just for the purpose of "getting together"'. In the event, 400 pupils attended the service in May, and were entertained to lunch, divided between the Hall and the Guildhall.[58] By the later 1970s the need for more regular contact was recognised. In 1976 it was agreed to invite to tea parties of 25 pupils from Hatcham and Elstree Boys' schools, and a reception for the teaching staff of the same schools was held.[59]

However, it was only under the Clerkship of Michael Barrow that a systematic effort was made to foster connections with all the schools, as the rhetoric of the Haberdasher family was extended beyond the confines of the Livery to the wider groups which the Haberdashers served. Each of the schools was encouraged to send 30-40 pupils each year on fixed days to be shown around by the Archivist and the Beadle and entertained to tea by the Clerk and his staff, a programme of school visits which has since been expanded. There were also successive receptions for the teaching staff of Elstree, Adams, and Monmouth in 1986-8, and in 1994 another series of receptions was arranged to give the staff at all the schools the opportunity to visit the Hall.[60] The Company has also used school anniversaries to foster its relationship. In the immediate post-war years its involvement was perhaps token. When Hatcham

74 The Aske's Schools' Tercentenary Float in the Lord Mayor's Show, 1990.

Boys celebrated its 75th anniversary in 1951, only a few Haberdashers turned up to the light-hearted pageant that the school put on. By contrast, the Aske Tercentenary in 1990 was marked by the sponsoring of a scientific expedition to Newfoundland, further entertainment of the school pupils and staff and a service in St Paul's attended by 2,250 people (including 1,800 pupils from the four schools) in the presence of H.R.H. The Princess Margaret.[61] Haberdashers' Monmouth School for Girls celebrated its centenary two years later, when the Company hosted three lunches at the Hall for staff and pupils, and provided mementoes for all pupils.[62] The 400th anniversary in 1994 of the foundation of Bunbury School was marked by a pageant of the school's history (again witnessed by H.R.H. The Princess Margaret) and a service of thanksgiving attended by 700 who heard an impressive sermon by the Rt Rev. Michael Baughen, Bishop of Chester, later invited to become a Liveryman Honoris Causa.[63]

Another important development has been the encouragement of shared activities between the schools, although successes have been mixed. Ned Goddard, Headmaster of Hatcham Boys and an enthusiast for joint events between the Aske schools, recalls the difficulties he encountered in the 1950s. The parties for sixth formers were more keenly supported by Hatcham, and met with a lukewarm response at Hampstead, and he was rebuffed in efforts to promote a rugby fixture. 'Nominally', he remarks, 'the four schools might appear to be equal, but some were more equal than others.'[64] Other problems arose from the suspicions generated by fraternisation between boys and girls.

75 Fancy Dress Ball for the Bunbury quatercentenary celebrations in 1994, featuring Mrs Judith Liddiard, Mr Michael Liddiard (Fourth Warden), Mrs Judy Barrow, Captain Michael Barrow, Mrs Val Bateman and Dr Christopher Bateman (Second Warden).

Eileen Harold, the traditionally-minded Headmistress at Acton (1944-68) had enforced the rule that no girl should speak to a male whilst wearing her school uniform, unless he was a member of her immediate family. She had responded to the discussions about a possible relocation of the school in the 1960s by considering a range of sites suitably remote from the boys' school now established at Elstree (she was keen on a site between Uxbridge, Denham, and Chalfont St Giles on the Buckinghamshire/Middlesex border).[65] Since their time, things have changed, as social mores have changed and the Company has lent its own weight to inter-school co-operation. The Haberdashers' Music Festival of 1986, the brainchild of Christopher Bostock, was so successful that it was decided to make it an annual event, but curricular pressures meant that it was scaled back to a biennial event from 1992, and from 1996 organised on an ad hoc basis.[66] Sporting competitions between the schools continue to be encouraged. The Fraser Bird seven-a-side rugby is a long-standing fixture; the Haberdasher Four begun in 2001 and, replacing the former Tripartite Sports Day, brings together pupils from the girls' schools for swimming, tennis, athletics, and netball competitions.[67] Co-operation has begun to be more common among school staff: Heads of Department at the different schools are encouraged to talk to each other. Hatcham's expertise in I.T. was put to good use by Adams in developing its Technology School status, and by Haberdashers' Monmouth School for Girls in reviewing its I.T. provision.[68]

What difference does it make to the schools that they are 'Haberdasher' schools? The answer, of course, varies. One variable is money. The resources

76   The Monmouth Schools' May Ball.

of the Aske foundation are much less than that of Jones. At the Monmouth schools, the resources of the charity are critical in keeping the fees at a level which can be afforded in a predominantly agricultural catchment area. In 2000, 30 per cent of the parents of Monmouth pupils had family incomes of less than £25,000.[69] At Elstree, the financial subsidy is smaller, and it is probably true to say that the schools there would now be successful irrespective of the foundation income. However, it should be borne in mind that the Company was a key motor behind the move to Elstree in the first place, which enabled the schools to embark on their virtuous spiral of upward academic success. For the schools in the state sector, the Company's insistence on the distinctive character of its schools has been a key factor in ensuring the survival of Adams; the conversion of Hatcham to C.T.C. status would have been inconceivable without the dogged resolve of Christopher Bostock and the commitment provided by the Company. At a time when school Governors have greater responsibilities, the Company's ability to draw upon a pool of talented, committed, and experienced people is a key factor in maintaining high standards of governance. Haberdasher Governors with experience of a variety of schools and a long-term commitment can perhaps mitigate some of the worst effects of the 'short-termism' to which parent Governors are occasionally prone. In no sense can Haberdasher Chairmen of Governors be described as 'faceless accountants'. Men like Tony Twiston-Davies (Livery, 1946, Master, 1981), long serving Chairman of the Monmouth Governors, have been able to bring a wealth of experience to the job: he had seen wartime service in the Navy, going on to become an eminent farmer in Wales, a collector of miniatures, a racehorse owner, and Chairman of the National Gallery of

Wales. David Sime and Dick Liddiard, though of contrasting styles, were towering influences at Elstree. All Haberdasher school Heads comment on the support they have received from the Company. Graeme Walker, Headmaster of Hatcham Boys from 1979, for example, talks of the support he received from five very distinguished Chairmen of Governors (Sir Maurice Bathurst, Owen Swingland, Gordon Bourne, Christopher Bostock, and Mark Powell), of how important Haberdasher support was in reconciling the school's old guard to the switch to comprehensive status, and of how Bostock shielded him from the day-to-day strife of the battles over C.T.C. status (as he puts it, 'running the school with a blitz going on over my head').[70]

It would be wrong to suggest that the relationship between the Company and the schools has been entirely stress-free. We have already observed how building projects could strain relationships, and behind that lies occasional misunderstanding over the resources of the charities. Local participants have not always enjoyed a realistic assessment of the wealth of the charities: it was quite clear, for example, that the local proponents of independent status for Adams in the 1970s were working under an illusory notion of the resources of the charity.[71] Even in the case of a wealthier trust like Jones, the schools and local interests have not always understood the necessity of maintaining the capital, to which the Company as trustee is committed. In 1991-2 and again in 1996 relations with the Monmouth Governors were strained when the Company pressed the case for the Governors being less dependent on the endowment income, and local interests felt that the Company was seeking to dictate terms. Relations have since improved, and in 1997 the Company guaranteed an income of £1.9 million per annum, rising by £125,000 per annum to £2.25 million in 2002-3, but this proved difficult to achieve as stock markets fell, and leaner years will undoubtedly lie ahead.[72] It is to be hoped that the difficulties will be more easily navigated. There is now far more transparency about finances, and the recent restructuring of the Education Committee represents an attempt to promote a better communication flow between the schools and the Hall.[73]

The Company has endeavoured not to 'micro-manage' the schools, most Chairmen of Governors admitting that the key decision they have taken is the appointment of a Head, and that an able Head will be able to carry his Governors with him. The Chairman's role is to 'encourage, advise, and warn'. But there are a couple of areas where the Company has intervened, ruffling feathers in the process. One has been a drive to ensure more co-operation between the schools and the pairings of schools. In 1969 the Company requested that serious consideration be given to the provision of a co-educational sixth-form at Monmouth, expressing indignation at the way the proposal had been dismissed out-of-hand at the Girls' School. As the minute notes, 'the Company having been in the forefront of educational affairs for more than three hundred years, they deprecated the implication that they should await the experience of other educational foundations instead of taking the initiative themselves'. They invoked their financial muscle, refusing to sanction any major building projects until the matter had been investigated.[74] The Heads were able to see

77   The Governors of Adams Grammar School in 1990.

the proposal off, but the issue of more shared activities was one which the Haberdashers continued to press energetically. It was soon on the agenda at Elstree too. There had been some reluctance on the part of the Acton establishment to move side-by-side with the Boys' School and, during the planning of the new Girls' School in 1972, Sir Maurice Bathurst and Sir Ian Bowater pressed for more shared facilities, but were firmly resisted by the Heads. As the schools settled down there was indeed more co-operation particularly in music and drama, but increasingly the success of the Girls' School contributed to the sense that it could perfectly well stand on its own feet.[75] The issue is one which crops up regularly from time to time at deputations. But the issues are by no means as straightforward as they at first might appear. One might assume, for example, that shared swimming facilities at Elstree would result in an economy of scale, but in fact the sheer size of both the schools means that one pool would not be sufficient.

The other area where sensitivities have been aroused in the past is religious education. The Haberdashers, as we have seen, are conscious of their christian heritage, and that can pose potential problems in running schools in an increasingly multi-faith and multi-ethnic society. The issue of the nature of religious education and specifically of the quality of christian knowledge could all too easily become entangled with the question of ethnic composition and quotas. When some Court members (among them John Denza, Livery, 1953, and Geoffrey Fox) pressed for information on ethnic composition at Elstree Boys in 1985, the Headmaster firmly resisted, and he carried his Chairman of Governors, Dick Liddiard, with him. Headmaster Bruce McGowan felt that the school's success depended on admission by academic ability only, and he did not want to have anything to do with quotas.[76] The question was raised again in 1987 when Fox was Master. Although some Court members were pressing

78   Sir Alan Traill, Lord Mayor, Mr Bruce McGowan (Headmaster) and
the Master, Mr Gordon Bourne at the opening of the new Sports Hall
at Elstree Boys' School, 1985.

for action on the content of the R.I. syllabus, it was decided to adopt a less
interventionist position and provide for the distribution of the King James'
version of the Bible to every pupil at every Haberdasher school, 'as a token
of the Company's past and present role as trustee of the school's foundation
and in recognition of its christian heritage'. Doubts were expressed by Gordon
Bourne and Twiston-Davies who felt that relations between the Company and
its schools might be compromised. Geoffrey Fox explained that the 'intention
was not to proselytise but that the Bible might remind pupils now and in the
future that they were part of a christian tradition'. Nevertheless it was decided
that the manner of distribution of Bibles should be left to the discretion of
individual school Heads. The practice is now a well established one, and
conducted with regard to the religious sensibilities of those of other faiths: the
King James' Bible after all is an extraordinary work of literature.[77]
    A variety of mechanisms has developed in recent years to defuse the tensions.
The reformed Education Committee with its permanent Chairman and two or
three members with experience as school Governors has sought to establish
better relations between the Company, the Governors, and the Heads. There is
a clearer appreciation on the part of the Company of a distinction between its

79 Publication 2002. The Master, The Hon. L.B. Hacking, with
Head Teachers and Head Pupils at the foot of the staircase.

role as trustee and the Governors' responsibilities for standards. The Assistant
Clerk for Schools performs a valuable function in behind-the-scenes discussions
with Heads and senior school management to ensure that the ground has been
well prepared for meetings, preventing them turning into 'stand-offs' between
entrenched positions. The Educational Adviser can assist the Company in
formulating policy sensitive to school needs as well as guiding the schools through
the turbulent waters of curriculum reform and government regulation.[78]

The Schools are in a healthy state at the turn of the millennium. The
Company can rightly claim that it has fostered their distinctive identity and
worked to establish frameworks within which their educational standards can
rise. The breadth of the Company's experience in the educational sector
derives from the variety of types of school it runs. Far from having acted
as a brake on change, sometimes the Company has been ahead of more
conservative opinion (for example on co-operation between schools) in the
schools themselves. Having taken a leading role in the C.T.C. initiatives, it
has remained committed to educational innovation, taking advantage of New
Labour's enthusiasm for specialist schools to secure Adams' future. Its mix of
schools gives it great potential in the developing area of public-private educational

80   Monmouth: Agincourt Pre-Prep School.

partnerships. Nor is it content to rest on its laurels, but has begun to seek out new educational partnerships. In 1996 the Company renewed contact with the West Monmouthshire School at Pontypool (it had surrendered the school to the County Council in 1955), and in the following year offered a pump-priming grant of £10,000 to provide support for further training in sports, music, and the arts, as well as advice from Aske College on information technology; since then there have been more exchanges and shared activities with the Monmouth schools.[79] In 1997 the Jones charity took over the pre-preparatory Agincourt School in Monmouth, to which it had previously provided occasional support. Several members of the Court feel that the Company should put its accumulated expertise to further use by taking over a failing school. There were abortive negotiations with the Lewisham L.E.A. over the possibility of the Haberdashers taking over a struggling comprehensive, Hatcham Wood School in 1998, which came to nothing. Subsequently there may be an opportunity to strengthen the Haberdashers' contribution to education in Lewisham by forming federated Haberdasher Academies, one at Hatcham College and the other at Malory School, the management of which would be taken over by Hatcham.[80] Education remains central to the Haberdashers' charitable mission, and the Company's willingness to reflect on its educational role places it well to participate in new initiatives.

Chapter Seven

From Staining Lane to Smithfield: The Company's Halls

The story of the Company's Hall in the later 20th century is to a considerable extent one of continuing frustration for, until the move to the West Smithfield site, there had been a long period of dissatisfaction with the facilities of the post-war Hall, and a series of abortive efforts to expand it. It was perhaps easy to criticise the Court of Assistants of the immediate post-war period for the haste with which they embarked upon the rebuilding project – the Haberdashers were the first of the companies whose Hall had been destroyed to rebuild, and the abrasive personality of E.A. Last-Smith (Livery, 1906, Master, 1951), seen by many as the driving force behind the project, caused one member of the Court, Lt. Col. John Bamford-Smith (Livery, 1907, Master, 1952), to resign over it in 1955 – leaving the Company with cramped and (externally, at any rate) architecturally unimpressive quarters, as well as for a long time a limited income flow from the office block which dominated the Hall complex.

Such a judgement is perhaps unfair because it fails to appreciate the difficulties of the planning and financial situation in the decade after the ending of the war. As long as the site remained undeveloped the Company was leaving a potential income-generating asset idle. Moreover, there was pressure to come up with plans to develop the site because of the threat of a compulsory purchase order by the City Corporation, seeking to replace the pre-war pattern of haphazard development with more strategic zoning and the development of blocks of property. In late 1947 the Company learned that the Corporation was planning to compulsorily purchase the Hall site and moved swiftly to launch an appeal against the decision. The Corporation's threat was lifted when the Haberdashers made clear their serious intention of acquiring the adjacent freeholds to sponsor an office development of which the new Hall would be part.[1] But immediate development was held up by the very tight post-war building restrictions, and by the need for the Corporation to wait for the submission of the L.C.C.'s plan for London. In any event it was dangerous for the Company to commit itself to any one scheme, given the extremely uncertain state of the demand for office property, not least because it remained unclear what the designated zoning of the area of the Hall would be – one should remember that in the pre-war period the area immediately north of the Hall had been an area of major textile warehouses, and if that were to remain the case the likely rent flow would be lower.[2] Nor should one forget the very real threat of renewed war in 1950-1, and the way in which this fuelled uncertainties about the future. When drawing up their initial specification for their new Hall it was remarked, somewhat optimistically, that its roof should be atomic blast proof and provide protection against the radiological effects of an air burst![3]

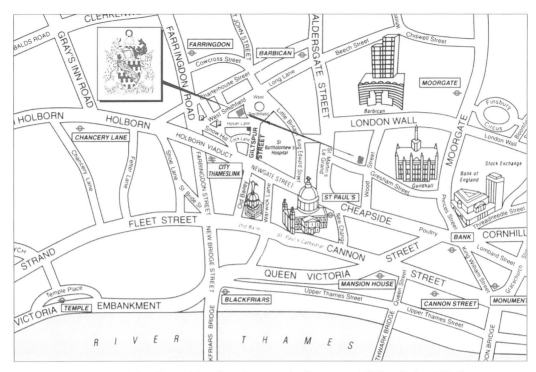

81   Map of the City of London showing the location of Haberdashers' Halls.

It was the speculative nature of the scheme which meant that the Company could not undertake the development of the site on its own. When building restrictions were lifted in 1950, the Company, still mindful of the possibility of a compulsory purchase order, sought a developer for the block surrounding the Hall, admittedly now a rather smaller unit than had been envisaged in 1947-8. It had originally been intended to develop the whole site between Gresham Street and Oat Lane, but this proved beyond the Company's capacity. It was still necessary to purchase land owned by the Grocers' Company, and a further strip from the Durning Lawrence Estates. This latter strip of just 1,900 square feet cost £11,000, and 1,600 square feet had to be handed back to the City Corporation for the widening of Wood Street. The Company protested vigorously, but it was made clear that unless the Company purchased the additional land permission to rebuild would be denied. In 1950 the Master on his own initiative approached Edwin McAlpine, who put him in touch with the architect Major Arthur Ash, who undertook to produce plans at no expense to the Company. In early 1951 the Company had found a potential developer in the form of Civic Leases Ltd., who undertook to lease the site and to arrange for the construction of an office block into which the Hall would be integrated.[4] Renewed building restrictions announced by the Chancellor of the Exchequer in June 1951 delayed the grant of a building licence, and

82 Construction of Garrard House, incorporating the Hall, 24 December 1954.

although the Company appealed on the grounds of the importance of its Hall as a centre for the administration of charity, and sought to mobilise its friends on the City Corporation through Alderman Sir Frederick Wells (Livery, 1942, Master, 1955), the licence was not secured until Easter 1954.[5] In the meantime financial backing was obtained from Legal and General Assurance Ltd though the Company was still uncertain about how much it would secure by way of a cost of works claim from the War Damages Commission, with whom negotiations ground on until April 1955.[6]

As the new office block incorporating the Hall rose from the rubble, Londoners came to gawp at the enormous crane being used by the builder McAlpine's, the first of its kind to be seen in the capital.[7] Apart from teething problems with the crane, the project seems to have been free from difficulties, and the Hall was completed in June 1956. Its cost was £139,485 7s. 9d. (with a further £15,738 for furnishings and equipment), and was met largely by the war damages payment of £113,750. The Rebuilding Fund largely from donations and bequests provided a further £13,901 7s. 5d., so the burden on corporate funds was kept to a minimum. The decision to seek a cost of works claim (as opposed to a value payment) from the War Damages Commission severely limited the scale of the new building, as its space could not exceed that of the old Hall. It had been hoped that the Hall could take over the ground floor and first floor of the main site of Garrard House, but it had emerged that this would cause problems with the War Damages Commission. From the outset the Company knew that it really needed more space.[8]

The Hall was opened by the Lord Mayor, Sir Cuthbert Ackroyd Bt. (he was the third choice: the Company had wanted H.R.H. The Princess Margaret or Winston Churchill) on 28 June 1956. After prayers by the Chaplain, and a speech of welcome by the Master, the Lord Mayor declared the Hall open. There was then a psalm by a choir from the schools and a blessing by the Rt Hon. and Rt Rev. D.H. Crick, Bishop of London. All members of the Court were required to attend in morning coats. There was a cocktail reception for 200, with subsequent parties for the schools, the builders, and three Livery Dinners.[9]

The negotiations with the architect suggest that many in the Company wanted something that would as far as possible replicate the recently destroyed Hall, though they were sometimes frustrated by considerations of economy. It had originally been hoped to incorporate the old chapel in the basement, the only part of the old Hall to escape serious damage in the Blitz, but this proved incompatible with maximising income from the new office building.[10] There were new features in the rather cramped but elegant entrance lobby lined with Trani marble, and bearing a plaque outlining the Hall's history. More conventional was the Livery Hall measuring 60ft by 30ft by 30ft and panelled in English oak according to a design based on the old Hall. Its decorative features encapsulated the Company's sense of continuity with the past, the centrality of charity to its self-presentation, and its close ties with Corporation and Crown.[11] The reproduction of the coats of arms of Past Masters was considered too expensive, and this honour was confined to previous Haberdasher Lord Mayors.[12] Around the walls were placed portraits of the key Haberdasher benefactors, some former Haberdasher Lord Mayors, and the royal portraits of George I and Queen Caroline. Above the latter was placed the Company's carved coat of arms presented by the Wardens in 1613, rediscovered in a Wembley antique shop in 1953, and given to the Company by E.A. Last-Smith.[13] The original idea to have a portrait of the new Queen was abandoned in favour of a portrait, copied from one by Sir A.S. Cope and owned by the United Grand Lodge of Freemasons of England, of the former Haberdasher Prince H.R.H. The Duke of Connaught, seventh child of Queen Victoria.[14] Stained glass windows in the minstrels' gallery decorated with arms of Jones, Adams, and Aske were presented by the schools. The chairs (costing 18 guineas each) in blue hide with padded backs carried the Company's arms stamped in gold.[15] Against the north wall stood the Lord Mayor's mace and sword stands. Elements of Haberdasher iconography surfaced elsewhere in the Hall complex. The Court Room was provided with a hand-loomed Wilton carpet incorporating the Company's coat of arms and bordered with a leaf and roundel band showing a series of Catherine wheels (in honour of the Company's patron saint).[16] The newel post of the Honduras mahogany staircase was topped with a heraldic goat carved by the wife of an Assistant, Mrs F.E. Tudor. She was also responsible for the carving of the cabinet with a table of subscribers to the new Hall paid for by Col W.R. Glover (Livery, 1905, Master, 1949) and matching the record of subscribers to the Hall built after the Great Fire: these initially graced the Court Room, but were later moved to the Committee Room.[17]

Other decoration owed a great deal to the combination of searches among antique dealers and the generosity of leading Company members. The Luncheon Room, one of the most attractive features of the old Hall, was panelled with Canadian waxed pine (*c*.1730) incorporating two pedimented door cases and a fine carved chimney piece, all from Clifton House in Brentford. The chandelier in the Luncheon Room was provided by the architect, Major Ash. In the Court Room the mahogany Court table was presented by Past Master R.H. Powell (Livery, 1896, Master, 1943) and his wife, who also donated the ornate looking-glasses; the chiming long-case clock dating to *c*.1700 was given by Past Master W.F. Dyer.[18] A silver standing cup was commissioned to commemorate the opening of the new Hall from Gerald Benney. A Loving Cup was given by W.B. Franklin (Livery, 1916, Master, 1957): it had originally been given to his grandfather Alderman Sir J.C. Bell (Master, 1912).[19]

Members were largely satisfied with the Hall in its early years, though the constraints of space were being felt as early as 1962 when the Company was discussing the possibilities of an extension into Garrard House; six years later the notion of building an additional storey on top of the Livery Hall was being explored, but considerations of cost and doubts about planning consents put off any major initiative.[20] There was more controversy about the use of lay lighting in the Livery Hall with many preferring the traditional chandeliers. In 1964 consultants were called in, but advised strongly against replacing the lay lighting which was an integral feature of the Hall's design. Nevertheless it was one of those issues which would not go away, and in 1969 the advocates of chandeliers finally got their way: the five chandeliers were donated by individual members of the Court.[21] Occasional modifications to the decorative scheme were made, as when in 1969 the Company commissioned copies of a late 17th-century decorative design bearing the Haberdasher coat of arms, and used it as a pattern for the wallpaper in the Committee Room, for which at the same time E.T.W. Dodd (Livery, 1922, Master, 1960) donated six silver wall sconces.[22] Financial constraints meant that new artistic commissions were rare. In 1966 it was agreed that the Company should aim to commission a new piece of plate worth £500 approximately every ten years; in 1982 the painting by G.S. Newton, *Yorrick and Griselde*, was purchased, and in 1986 paintings of four recent Haberdasher Lord Mayors who had also served as Master (Sir Frederick Wells, Sir Cullum Welch, Sir Gilbert Inglefield, and Sir Ian Bowater) were commissioned from Jeffrey Courtney.[23] In 1983 a Fine Arts Committee was established under the Chairmanship of Tony Twiston-Davies, though some more hard-bitten Court members doubted its utility; Christopher Bostock, one of its members, told fellow Assistants after a decade of the committee's functioning that 'it had no money to spend but [its members] had great fun while conducting its business'.[24]

By 1980 the constraints of space were more keenly felt and there was mounting pressure to expand the available accommodation and office space. The Clerk's flat consisted of one small bedroom, the Beadle's flat was cramped, the reception rooms for visitors were inadequate, there was no drawing room for members of the Court or visitors, and no rest room for staff.[25] The renegotiation of the Garrard House lease with Legal and General in 1982 offered some opportunities, both because of the improved income flow and because the Company obtained a premium of £250,000 which was earmarked for the expansion of the Hall. For some time the Court energetically explored the possibility of building the additional storey to provide extra accommodation and thereby release office space on the second floor. In October 1983 £424,700 was earmarked for the project, albeit in the face of some opposition on the Court on the grounds that the cost was out of all proportion to the gain. The sceptics were proved correct, for the additional requirements of the Fire Officer eroded the available space on the projected new floor, and the advice of the structural engineers was that the building structure would not accommodate the additional loading; the project was both financially and practicably non-viable.[26] Thereafter the possibility of a break through into Garrard House was again explored but inconclusively, partly because of Legal and General's lack of clarity about the future of the office block, but also because of a combination of financial and aesthetic doubts. Meanwhile the Master's flat was refurbished and a lease taken on part of the basement area from Legal and General to create space for wine storage, but these measures hardly addressed the core problem.[27]

By late 1986 the prospects for a redevelopment of the whole Garrard House site seemed rosier, and Legal and General were apparently more enthusiastic; a Hall Redevelopment Committee was set up. As negotiations proceeded tensions emerged between the Company's dual objectives of improved revenue and an enhanced Hall. It was recognised that either a substantial part of the Hall would need to be below ground level, or that an alternative site for a free-standing Hall elsewhere in the City should be sought. Several Court members were profoundly uneasy about the prospect of a subterranean existence (and the idea of moving the site of the Hall was first mooted at this time), but the Court did agree in June 1987 to negotiate with Legal and General in a scheme envisaging just such a possibility.[28] The scheme proposed was subject to a number of factors that made its viability difficult to demonstrate. These included the cost penalty of building several storeys below ground level; the need to provide the Haberdashers' accommodation, even below ground level, with sufficient open aspects and daylighting; and the ratio of net office floor space to gross building space. Moreover, the boom in city rentals meant that the value of Legal and General's leasehold interest had risen, casting further doubts on the viability of the scheme.[29] Harold Quitman's Property Committee, looking at the possibilities of working with more 'bullish' developers, kept up the pressure on Legal and General, who did produce revised plans in 1989 for which they were ready to seek outline planning consent. But the economic climate was less favourable to office development, and again they withdrew.[30] Meanwhile, the expiration of the sub-leases having passed in 1990, the Company was left in the worst possible position: much of the very dated office space was now untenanted, and the rental income declined markedly. The fact that the Company was running a deficit made it impossible for it to exercise its option (agreed in 1982) of taking over part of the ground floor of Garrard House that was under consideration after the vacation of that floor by the previous occupying tenant in 1990-1992.[31]

It had been a very frustrating few years and for some time relations with Legal and General were strained, but they were restored by the end of 1992. The Company was careful to encourage Legal and General into not granting sub-leases beyond 1995 in the hope that prospects for development would improve, as indeed turned out to be the case; the Hall Redevelopment Sub Committee was reactivated at the end of 1993.[32] But there was a tortuous round of negotiations ahead as the Company, Legal and General, Hill Samuel (potential tenants of the new office block), and Wates Ltd. (property developers) wrangled. Wates had a more ambitious scheme for a development of 295,000 square feet taking in the sites of Garrard House, Hill Samuel's building at 100 Wood Street, and Hamersley House (Jones Charity property) at 90/91 Wood Street to the north. Some consideration was given to a proposal in the context of this scheme for a new Hall approximately on the site of 90/91 Wood Street, but it was not pursued.[33] The critical decision to seek an alternative site for the Hall was taken on 31 May 1995 with surprising ease; it was recognised that to remain on the historic site would compromise the revenue flow from the new building. Meanwhile, however, the Wates scheme faltered because of the reluctance of Hill Samuel to move within the required time frame, and Legal and General went ahead on the basis of more modest proposals for an office development of 125,000 square feet on the existing Garrard House site.[34]

The negotiations were complex. It was necessary to secure the co-operation of Hill Samuel to permit the blocking of their windows in 100 Wood Street, which looked out over the car park of Garrard House and over the top of the old Hall. Hill Samuel were reluctant to agree terms with Legal and General without at the same time agreeing terms with the Haberdashers for the purchase of the Company's freehold interest in Hamersley House from the Company's Charity Pool. By this time Hamersley House was a poorer quality investment because it was still let for the balance of a 99-year lease from the 1950s, and the rent reviews took place only every 14 years and were based on the original specification of the building. The proposed redevelopment enabled the Company's advisers, Keith Way and Philip Edwards of D.T.Z. Debenham Thorpe, to drive a hard bargain, selling the property for £5.5 million in 1997.[35]

By June 1996 the Haberdashers and Legal and General were ready to agree terms. A key component was a £9 million capital payment which would be available for a new Hall, but there was also the prospect of a much improved revenue stream from the rebuilt Garrard House: 9.5 per cent of rents received would from 1998 produce an annual income of at least £571,000 per annum.[36] By October 1996 the Haberdashers had vacated the historic Staining Lane site, embarking on what was to be a five-and-a-half-year sojourn in temporary office

83   The Company's temporary offices, 39/40 Bartholomew Close.

accommodation in Bartholomew Close, hard by the church of St Bartholomew the Great and the Founders' Hall, while its social functions continued at other Company Halls hired for the occasion.[37]

It had not been intended to be quite so long a wait. With what seems in retrospect heady optimism a project timetable drawn up in early 1997 envisaged a design proposal by June, a detailed design by January 1998, commencement of construction in mid-1998, and completion in early 2000.[38] In the event the new Hall was completed two years later than that. Things went initially to plan. The Company had considered a variety of sites for a relocated Hall, including the adaptation of part of the old Public Record Office in Chancery Lane, the conversion of various redundant banking halls in the City, adaptation of the old City Livery Club and adjoining offices on the Embankment, and even development sites in Aldersgate Street. It had been known for a while that the site of Weddel House in West Smithfield might come onto the market because of the expiry of long leases in 1997, and the need for the freeholders, the Special Trustees of Saint Bartholomew's Hospital, to improve their investment, whether by participating in a development of the site, or through sale and reinvestment elsewhere. Because the Haberdashers knew that their proposals for the site would meet, in principle, with City Corporation approval in accordance with the planning policies for the area, they were one of the few parties who could offer the Special Trustees a transaction that did not have to be conditional upon securing a planning consent. As a result the Company was able to negotiate a purchase, exchanging contracts on 24 January 1997, although with completion postponed until such time as the Special Trustees were able to deliver vacant possession which was secured in July 1997.[39]

West Smithfield is one of those fascinating quarters of the City, dominated by the meat market and by the hospital, retaining more of its pre-war building stock than many other areas, for a long time out of fashion, but now undergoing something of a renaissance, so that greasy spoon cafés sit cheek by jowl with Carluccio's fashionable café restaurant. The original Weddel House dated from 1884 and it was substantially extended in the early 20th century, eventually coming to house the offices and refrigeration spaces of Vesteys, the meat wholesalers.[40] Although initially the Haberdashers had envisaged pulling down Weddel House, and building a new Hall on the entire site, considerations of cost meant that it was soon recognised that it would be necessary to redevelop or refurbish Weddel House, and build in the space behind. The site had many complications: rights of light agreements with adjoining owners; an irregular rear boundary to the adjoining City Corporation site, which suggested the need for an exchange of land to straighten the alignment; the need to remove substantial amounts of asbestos from Weddel House itself; the need for licences to permit a tower crane to oversail neighbouring properties; and the elimination of former rights of fire escape over the site. The purchase was thus one of considerable complexity.[41]

The site was the first essential. The second was an architect. Taking the advice of Marcus Binney, architectural correspondent of *The Times*, the Company decided to hold a 'beauty contest' of architects, interviewing six hopefuls in May 1996, and adopted Sir Michael Hopkins, the architect of the new opera house at Glyndebourne, Portcullis House (the office accommodation for the Houses of Parliament), the Inland Revenue Headquarters at Nottingham, and the Fidelity development at Millharbour in the London Docklands. Hopkins' appeal over his rivals lay in his sensitivity to the mixed use of the site, his understanding of the needs of a Livery Company, and his excitement at the prospect of taking a piece of late Victorian London and transforming it by blending ancient and modern idioms.[42] Negotiations with Hopkins were conducted by the Hall Project Team established early in 1997 and presided over by a veteran of Hall redevelopment discussions, Sir Brian Jenks, and assisted by the property experts Peter Davidson and Michael Wheldon, Brian Shawcross (representing the Fine Arts Committee), and Julien Prevett (Livery, 1962, Master, 2003).[43] The Hall Project Team performed two functions: first, the Court of Assistants delegated supervision of design to avoid, consciously or unconsciously, the myriad of opinions that might arise between 45 Assistants; and second, to oversee all aspects of development by monthly meetings with the Project Manager, architects, engineers, quantity surveyors, and contractors.[44]

The brief prepared in 1997 was for buildings of brick and stone around a courtyard in the manner of a grand country house. Hopkins' first draft of his design (about 40,000 square feet instead of the 24,000 square feet as finalised) had to be shelved because of the need to maximise the residential space. There was a good deal of toing-and-froing between architect and client over the details before a revised design was approved in October 1998, and thereafter a lot of debate over materials (especially in view of the cost considerations) and over details of the interior decoration. Hopkins' design concept found wide approval, though inevitably there were disagreements as to where the point of balance between the modern and traditional should lie. The Courtyard feature

84   The Architect's model for the new Hall.

was enthusiastically endorsed (with admittedly one or two dissentient voices who felt it wasteful of space), the pitched Livery Hall roof was recognised early on as an exciting and original feature; there was more anxiety about the stainless steel tie beams of the Hall ceiling, and it required much patient exposition by Hopkins' team to persuade some Court members that they were structurally essential. The Fine Arts Committee expressed a desire for features of the old Hall to be incorporated into the new building, but this was sometimes, as with the desire to make use of the Livery Hall panelling, at odds with the architect's simplicity of line. As pressures for economy mounted, it is important to realise, however, that the Hall Project Team stuck with Hopkins' core vision. When some Assistants pressed for the panelling in the reception gallery to be abandoned as too expensive, Jenks' committee wisely insisted that it be retained.[45]

More problematic, needless to say, was the financing. When the Company had secured the £8.6 million net premium for Garrard House, the hope was that this would not only pay for a new Hall but would also leave a surplus that could boost the corporate funds, enabling the Company to expand its range of charitable activities. This was too optimistic.[46] The acquisition cost of the West Smithfield site alone was £6.45 million; admittedly much of this would be recovered through the residential development of Weddel House, but the quest for a developer who would offer good terms was to be by no means straightforward, and contributed to some of the delays in the project. Negotiations with the Manhattan Loft Corporation (for a residential development incorporating Weddel House and the Hosier Lane site) dragged into the summer months of 1998 but without a satisfactory agreement, so the Company instructed

85 Weddel House, now Market View.

its property advisers D.T.Z. to seek new developers. By Christmas 1998 London and Henley had agreed to undertake the residential development of Weddel House for a premium of £5 million (£4.8 million after costs). Weddel House, now renamed Market View, and completed in mid-2001, provides 65 serviced appartments over ground floor retail units. All of the ground-floor and basement accommodation has been reserved back to the Company for letting.[47] Another set of difficult decisions pertained to the Hosier Lane site: first whether it should be another residential development or offices; and secondly, whether the Company should undertake the development itself. It was recognised that this would be to some extent a speculative development, though one of potential long-term benefit to the Company, but to defer development would significantly increase the costs in longer term. So in 2000 it was agreed to develop a six-storey office building on the Hosier Lane site, the project being financed partly by the sale of 37 Lombard Street which realised £2.115 million. The office space in Hosier Lane totals about 15,300 square feet with another 3,000 square feet of basement storage space.[48]

The cost of the Hall itself proved greater than had originally been envisaged. At the end of 1996 it has been expected that the costs of construction would be £3.5 million; by early 1998 when costings came to the Court this had risen to £4.8 million. Once fees, site costs (including demolition) and V.A.T. had been factored in, the funds required for the building of the Hall totalled £7.758 million.[49] This was already after the scaling back of the original specification to allow for greater residential development, but it meant that the total project costs were going to exceed the £9 million (the premium on the Garrard House redevelopment), which was for some Assistants the bottom line in assessing the

86 Laying of the foundation stone of the new Hall by Rt. Hon. the Lord Mayor, Alderman Clive Martin, 4 October 2000 with the Master, Mr Michael Wheldon.

87 The Master, Mr Brian Shawcross, brazing the Haberdasher coat of arms onto the 'chimney' at the topping out of the new Hall, 25 July 2001.

project's feasibility. In July 1997 therefore the Court of Assistants agreed that £1.5 million could be committed from corporate funds to meet an anticipated total project cost of £14.9 million (that is including the cost of acquiring the site, and funding for contingencies).[50] As the planning continued through 1998 costs rose further, not least because of the inflation of building costs (then running at 6 per cent per annum) but also because of the necessity for deeper and thicker foundations, but the recovery of VAT and modifications to Hopkins' design suggested that the project could be kept within budget.[51] It was with some horror therefore that the Company faced the results of the tendering process in November 1999, as the tenders for the construction of the Hall fell within the range of £10 million to £10.6 million, well beyond the estimate of £8.79 million.[52] This may have been because the tenderers were more nervous of the architect's requirements than the Quantity Surveyor (Robinson Low Francis) had anticipated. Holloway White Allom were appointed as builders (though not the cheapest they had an excellent reputation, and were thought likely to meet the building's very particular challenges), but there was a delay of a few months as it proved necessary to engage in a comprehensive value engineering survey to identify potential savings. With those involved working at full throttle (the design team had three full-day workshops) savings totalling £2.632 million were identified: for example, the use of a different type of brick on the unseen walls would save £395,000, the use of American rather than English oak would save £595,000. Of these proposed savings, 93 per cent were achieved by late summer 2000 bringing the construction costs to an estimated

88 Construction of the Hall, 2000/2001: brickwork rising.

89 Construction of the Hall, 2000/2001: the hydraulic rams on the Hosier Lane site.

£8.13 million as compared to the original contract price of £7.75 million.[53] The financial situation was perhaps not quite as gloomy as this rehearsal of the escalating costs suggests: the Garrard House redevelopment had boosted corporate income, and the investment portfolio had grown substantially up to 2000, but as the commitment from corporate funds mounted, it became clear that it was going to be necessary to market the new building aggressively for use by others to generate additional income.[54]

As with their previous Halls, the Haberdashers sought to mobilise the generosity of members to support the project. The Millennium Appeal raised a total of £775,000, of which £355,000 will come to the Millennium Treasures Trust supporting the new Hall, once all covenants are paid and tax is recovered. Twenty donations of over £10,000 were received, many from Assistants and several from leading Haberdasher families; there were another 199 donations of below £10,000. Nevertheless, the amounts raised were not equal to the project's enormous scale, nor do they compare favourably with the donations to the post-war Hall.[55]

Demolition works took place between August 1998 and January 1999; construction began on 24 January 2000, and the foundation stone was laid by the Lord Mayor Alderman Sir Clive Martin on 4 October 2000; topping out took place on 25 July 2001.[56] Hopkins' vision would not have been realised without the professionalism of Gardner Theobald, the Project Managers, who had worked recently on the post-fire restoration of Windsor Castle and who had prior experience of working with Hopkins. Guy Macauley of Gardner Theobald became the lynch-pin of the Design Team which dealt with the 'nitty gritty' problems on site, and reported to the Hall Project Team. Holloway White Allom's key man was Jim Dunn, who adopted a flexible and creative approach to the problems posed by the building. Although Sir Michael Hopkins had been closely involved with the building in its early stages, Jim Greaves was critical to the implementation of the design. Lady Hopkins took a keen interest in the project and attended the critical meetings; in the later stages Hopkins' son-in-law Amir Sanei and Tony White of the Hopkins practice were increasingly involved in the construction of the Hall and the Hosier lane offices. Monitoring the construction continued to consume an enormous amount of the time of the members of the Hall Project Team and the Clerk, Robert Fisher, as their secretary, who insulated the Court of Assistants from some of the tough decisions. The Company was particularly fortunate in the diplomatic skills of Sir Brian Jenks and in the property expertise of Peter Davidson. There were regular meetings with the architect's representatives and the contractors, often at breakfast time, and the pile of papers by Jenks' bedside grew to a height of four feet.[57]

The work of construction was exciting but not unproblematic. There were remarkable visions like the construction on site of the enormous lozenge-like lead panels for the roof. It was a complicated building made with high quality materials and posed novel and stimulating challenges to the contractors. There were inevitable hold-ups. It was difficult to co-ordinate the Hosier Lane office development with the Hall; bad weather caused delays (high winds restricted use of the crane on site; the sandpits which provided lime mortar for the brickwork were flooded by the overflowing of the Ouse early in 2001); there were glitches in communication between architect and contractors (some key drawings were not available until a later stage); the design of the panelling for the reception gallery was changed during installation; the use of traditional building materials sometimes caused problems (for example, the lime mortar used on the brickwork took much longer to reach the load-bearing strength necessary to support the structure, and in other cases the materials did not match the specification). Jim Dunn's ingenuity and patience proved invaluable in negotiating these difficulties. The delays were frustrating, especially as they had cost implications, but they were perhaps inevitable in view of the scheme's originality, the difficulties of the site, and the traditional materials being used in construction.[58]

The Staff made the move from Bartholomew Close to the new Hall in January 2002, and over the next few months the Company was able gradually to take over the public spaces. Even at this late stage there were frustrating delays: the lavatory fittings were not delivered from France on time, and the temperature controls were initially not effective. The first function at the new Hall, the Masters' and Clerks' Dinner, took place on 18 April just two days after the hand-over from the contractors. After a gap of five years the Company had its own home once more, and the cycle of meetings, dinners, receptions, and schools visits resumed on home ground, though there are more non-Company occasions as the building is being actively marketed for use by others for a variety of events.[59]

The Haberdashers' relationship with Hopkins may have had its ups and downs, but the result is a very striking building which makes a far bolder statement than the essentially conservative post-war Hall, and sets a new standard for Livery Company halls in the 21st century.[60] Hopkins' work picks up on traditional idioms but transforms them. He has explained, 'I set out to provide a building in the manner of an Oxford or Cambridge college, with a porter's lodge and just a glimpse of green from the street. Around the Courtyard is a colonnade part open like a loggia, part glazed in like a conservatory'. But he transcends the collegiate model in using the same elevations for the component parts, only indicating the centrality of the Livery Hall by its 45-degree pitched roof with its diamond grid of lead panels and the striking chimney louvres. The key public spaces, the Orangery with Reception Gallery above, and the Livery Hall, respond to the 20 metre square quadrangle dimensions, so that the Livery Hall (20 by 10 metres) forms a double square in relation to the Courtyard, while the Reception Gallery (20 by 5 metres) incorporates two five metre square lobbies defining the corners of the quadrangle. The result is an architectural promenade through the public spaces. The Reception Gallery and Livery Hall define two sides of the quadrangle; the other two are occupied by the more private spaces of the Library, the Drawing Room, and the flats for the Master and Beadle.

90   Livery Hall, 1956.

91   Livery Hall, 2002.

The Livery Hall itself is a triumph. The sash windows modelled on those in the Long Room at Lord's Cricket Ground create the effect of standing on a balcony. The windows have vertically folding 'Roman' blinds in deep blue silk and silver braid. The room is panelled in North American oak incised into panels and without the traditional cornices and projecting door frames. Hopkins provides a reinterpretation of the medieval hammer-beam roof, using diagonal rafters in place of traditional orthogonal roof trusses and cross bracing. The stainless steel tie rods which so exercised the Court at the design stage support the 85 tonne lead roof, and clever lighting manages to make them sparkle like silver. The ceiling, here as also in the Reception Gallery, repeats the lozenge pattern of the external roof.

The Meeting Rooms posed other challenges because the crowded nature of the surrounding site meant that these rooms lack a view, and rely upon clerestory lighting. This is most successful in the Court Room whose apsidal form matches the traditional semi-circular layout of tables for meetings. It is perhaps less successful in the Luncheon Room which incorporates the much-loved 18th-century panelling from the Luncheon Room at Staining Lane, where the combination of modern ceiling with traditional walls seems awkward.

The furnishings represent a blending of old and new.[61] The retention of links with the old Hall is inevitable for an organisation which prides itself on continuity. The Luncheon Room panelling is a case in point; whatever one makes of the overall conception of the room one has to admire the skill of crafting of a new section of panelling necessitated by the need to fill the former window spaces. The Kent fireplace from the old Binding Parlour is now in the Drawing Room. The original Court Room table donated by R.H. Powell (Master,1943) and his wife has been retained though restored and lightened in colour, and with five additional curved panels commissioned to ensure that it follows the contours of the room. The larger capacity of the new Livery Hall necessitated another 52 chairs, and it was decided to replicate the design of the old chairs though again lightening the wood. As in the 1950s, members were invited to subscribe to provide a chair, though the passage of nearly fifty years had seen the expected contribution rise from 18 guineas to £500. At the foot of the main staircase is the figurehead of Saint Catherine from the 17th-century barge. At the top of the staircase the visitor is greeted with the angel from the previous Meeting House, the carved coat of arms of Charles I, and the Company's bell dated 1804, probably originally from the hospital at Hoxton for almsmen and school children. The stained glass windows incorporating the arms of William Adams, William Jones, and Robert Aske have been installed at the south-east corner of the ground-floor cloister. The importance of the Company's civic connections is emphasised by the wrought-iron stands for the Lord Mayor's sword and mace which occupy a central place in the new Hall. The clock presented in 1714 by Sir Francis Forbes, Master in 1713 and Lord Mayor in 1726, hangs beneath the Minstrels' Gallery. The portraits of Haberdasher benefactors grace the new Livery Hall as they did the old, but Hopkins' economical lines should not be too cluttered!

92   Luncheon Room, 1956.

93   Luncheon Room, 2002.

New furniture has been commissioned for the Reception Gallery from Viscount Linley's firm, who consulted closely with Hopkins. There are four black granite-topped side tables in brown oak, two banquettes also in brown oak, and a half-moon Indian rosewood console table. All have recessed silver inlay panels. The Roger Lloyd Partnership provided bookcases, cupboards, and display cabinets for the Library and Exhibition Room. The Court Room has a new machine-woven blue carpet (produced by Tyndale's) including the gold Catherine wheel motif throughout, the Company's coat of arms, and the motto 'Serve and Obey' laid out before the Master. The same Catherine wheel motif is used in the carpeting for the Reception Gallery.

The building of a new Hall and the availability of money to spend with the establishment of the Haberdashers' Millennium Treasures Trust has reinvigorated the Fine Arts Committee, which became the Hall Committee with wider responsibilities in 2002. A variety of important new commissions has resulted. At the centre of a circle of York stone paving in the courtyard is a bronze water feature designed by the leading sculptor of water features, William Pye. It consists of a buttressed urn into which three jets of water are pumped and then spill down steps. The three jets represent the three methods of entry to the Company, by service, patrimony, and redemption. The contributions are collected in the bronze urn which represents the City of London from where they are distributed down steps representing the original trade in haberdashery, the governance of the City, the charitable works of the Company, and its religious origins.[62] Other works likewise serve to celebrate the continuity of the Company and its contribution to national and civic life. The large city panorama by Jeffrey Morgan, commissioned as early as 1994 but already with a new Hall in mind, now graces the wall of the ground-floor entrance lobby and shows the key 17th-century Haberdasher benefactors accompanied by H.R.H. The Princess Margaret and the Senior Past Master, Sir Robin Brook (with other intentionally less readily identifiable Haberdashers) on an imagined Haberdasher balcony transported to the Shakespeare Tower of the Barbican surveying the modern City towards St Paul's; the new Hall is visible. The artist's viewpoint, while more elevated, is not far removed from that of Charles Cundall, RA, whose painting of the bomb-damaged City before the reconstruction of the Staining Lane Hall hangs in the Luncheon Room.[63] The Orangery houses the boards of contributors to the successive Halls taken from the former Committee Room, but a new cabinet with supporting goats has been carved by Hugh Wedderburn to record the names of those who contributed to the Millennium Appeal. At Publication in 2003 a sundial was commissioned and mounted on the north wall of the courtyard to commemorate the 500th anniversary of the granting of the Company's heraldic shield. At the foot of the spiral staircase are two heraldic goats carved by Mary Beattie Scott, the wife and mother of Liverymen, and the daughter of Ernest Potter (Master, 1948). (Mrs Tudor's goat from the staircase of the old Hall sits on a table in the Reception Gallery upstairs.) Particularly striking are the stained glass windows commissioned from Peter Sutton in the new Committee Room. The Haberdashers' Window

94   The Court Room, 2002.

95   The Reception Gallery, 2002.

96   The Orangery, with examples of art from schools on display.

incorporates heraldic elements from the Company's coat of arms, the figure of
St Catherine (the Company's patron saint), a benefactor bearing a book and
a will, a figure reading to suggest the Company's connections with education,
and hands passing buttons and pins signifying the original craft origins and
the charitable work of the Company, and architectural features of historic city
sites with which haberdashery has been identified. The other window, donated
by the Feltmakers' Company which broke away from the parent Haberdashers
in 1604, illustrates the processes involved in traditional hat making (bowing
fur, brushing a cone-shaped hood, trimming a hat), and includes heraldic and
architectural motifs including London Bridge and the Millennium Wheel.

The building of the new Hall has also been an occasion for an important series
of silver commissions and gifts. The most important is the table centrepiece by
the leading jewellery designer and silversmith, Jocelyn Burton, paid for in large
part by contributions from the other 11 of the Great Twelve Livery Companies.
From the triangular base bearing the coats of arms of the Great Twelve (those of
the Haberdashers distinguished by their enamelled colouring) rise three heraldic
goats bearing a lapis lazuli bowl with a silver band representing a millennium
sky (specifically in homage to the Haberdashers, that of St Catherine's Day
2000). By way of response to the Millennium appeal and to commemorate four
generations of family association with the Company (commencing in 1889), the

97   Cabinet with names of donors to new Hall.

98   The Committee Room showing stained glass windows and tapestry.

99 Courtyard of new Hall, looking north and showing the water feature by William Pye.

Hiscocks family have donated a Loving Cup, developed from the designs for the 1992 Downing Street coffee set by Robert Welch, who died shortly before completion of the piece in 2000. Christopher Bostock has donated an art deco Loving Cup (*c*.1926) by Charles Boyton to record the admission of the three Bostock brothers to the Company in the 1920s and 1930s. Past Master Nicholas Wills (Livery, 1973, Master, 1997) has donated a rosewater dish designed by Stephen Canbury. Recognising a shortage of appropriate pieces for large dinners the Company has commissioned another two rosewater dishes and another Loving Cup. The designers were identified in association with the Goldsmiths' Company. Adrian Hope's rosewater dish makes allusions to the craft's origins: the bowl is made up of a dozen sections patterned in the texture of a coarse cloth to bring to mind 'hapertas', the cloth worn beneath chain mail which (on some accounts at least!) is the origin of the word 'haberdashery'. The younger artist Toby Russell has produced another dish and cup in a highly imaginative design: central to his concept is the way light describes the form as a moving element over curved and sweeping planes.

It is a sign of the times that the Hall can be toured virtually (and with an impressive 'zoom-in' and 'pan-out' facility) on the web site of Chester Boyd

100 Presentation of the Panorama of the City, 24 April 1997. Past Master Sir Robin Brook and HRH The Princess Margaret are pictured with Past Master Mr Christopher Bostock, Mr Jeffrey Morgan, the artist, and the Master, Dr Christopher Bateman.

Ltd., the caterers who initially have been given the task of marketing the building. To handle the greater volume of functions, for the first time in its history the Company has a permanent on-site kitchen staff, for from the earliest times catering for Livery Company functions was bought in. There will be a greater variety of functions in the new Hall, and more people will have a chance to view it, albeit perhaps at the expense of its unique function as the centre of Haberdasher fraternal life. The Hall's primary purpose is as a focus for the Haberdasher family, and it should have the effect of reinvigorating its corporate social life, and of enabling still closer relations with the Schools. There is no doubt that the new building offers enhanced facilities. The Display Room means that the Company will be able to show off its treasures more easily, while the Library and Sitting Room provide extra spaces for relaxation and study not enjoyed in the previous Hall.

The Hall was officially opened by Her Majesty the Queen on Thursday 24 October 2002 in the presence of 300 people. After a welcome by the Master and the Lord Mayor, and prayers by the Rev. Canon David Burgess, Chaplain to the Company, Her Majesty declared the Hall open and unveiled a plaque in the Entrance Hall. She was then given a tour of the Hall and an opportunity

101 Items of New Silver: (from left to right) the Millennium Bowl by Jocelyn Burton; Loving Cup and Rosewater Dish by Toby Russell.

102 Items of New Silver: (from left to right back row) The Bostock Loving Cup by Charles Boyton, lid by Beaulagh Sloan Chapman; The Wills Bowl by Stephen Canbury of Hancocks and Co., The Hiscocks Cup by Robert Welch; (front row) The Sturgess Butter Dishes by C.J. Vander Ltd; Rosewater Dish by Adrian Hope.

103   Her Majesty The Queen signing the Visitors' Book at the opening
of the new Hall, 24 October 2002.

to meet representatives of the various spheres of Haberdasher activity. The
Hall Project Team, Assistants, Liverymen, Freemen and Apprentices, the Heads
and pupils from the schools, representatives of the charities supported by the
Company and of the affiliated units of the Armed Services, were given allocated
standings around the Hall's public rooms, and Her Majesty was introduced
to about 100 individuals. The Queen was presented with a sketch portrait by
Jeffrey Morgan of the late H.R.H. The Princess Margaret who had been an
Honorary Liveryman and later Assistant Honoris Causa of the Company. The
Queen was also presented with a posy by two pupils of Aldersey Primary
School in Bunbury, Cheshire. The opening was an occasion which proudly
encapsulated the Company's vision of itself: a traditional body aligned with the
Crown, the Church, and the City of London, with a continuing key role in
education and charitable work, and a life and enjoyment of its own company
and wider family, all of which will continue and hopefully prosper for centuries
to come in its newly constructed fifth Hall.

Masters and Wardens, 1939-2003

	Master	First Warden	Second Warden	Third Warden	Fourth Warden
1939	R.L. Carter	Major E.A. Dodd	Alderman Sir Maurice Jenks	W.R. Wilkin	R.L. Moreton
1940	Major E.A. Dodd	Alderman Sir Maurice Jenks	Sir Gerald Wollaston	Stephen Bird	Rev. Canon T.G. Edwards
1941	Alderman Sir Maurice Jenks	Sir Gerald Wollaston	R.H. Powell	F.P. Coates	W.F. Dyer
1942	Sir Gerald Wollaston	R.H. Powell	J. Gibson Harris	Bernard Elliott	Dr. D.B.I. Hallett
1943	R.H. Powell	J. Gibson Harris	C.E. Fletcher	Lt. Cmdr. A.F. Inglefield	Rev. H.S. Shard
1944	J. Gibson Harris	C.E. Fletcher	F.E. Tudor	W.B. Franklin	B.G. Donne
1945	C.E. Fletcher	F.E. Tudor	R.R.L. James	P.C. Bull	A.S. Warren
1946	F.E. Tudor	R.R.L. James	E.H. Potter	R.W. Foot	Major H.E.D. Elliott
1947	R.R.L. James	E.H. Potter	Col. W.R. Glover	S.M. Pettitt	C.G. Gardner
1948	E.H. Potter	Col. W.R. Glover	A.W.C. Hamsher	Col. K.H.A. Gross	E.T.W. Dodd
1949	Col. W.R. Glover	A.W.C. Hamsher	E.A. Last-Smith	Lt. Col. C.W. Cronin	R.S. Blundell
1950	A.W.C. Hamsher	E.A. Last-Smith	Lt. Col. J. Bamford Smith	J.B. Perkins	R.T. Hawes
1951	E.A. Last-Smith	Lt. Col. J. Bamford Smith	W.R. Wilkin	Rev. A.W.G. Cope	Rt. Hon. Lord Moynihan
1952	Lt. Col. J. Bamford Smith	R.L. Moreton	W.F. Dyer	J.G. Carr	P.E.M. Shaw
1953	R.L. Moreton	W.F. Dyer	Alderman Sir Frederick Wells	M.O. Sheffield	R.E. Brook
1954	W.F. Dyer	Alderman Sir Frederick Wells	Bernard Elliott	Lt. Col. I.F. Bowater	P.B. Powell
1955	Alderman Sir Frederick Wells	Bernard Elliott	Dr. D.B.I. Hallett	Lt. Col. F.S. Bird	G.T. Bentley
1956	Bernard Elliott	W.B. Franklin	P.C. Bull	G.S. Inglefield	H.W. Wollaston
1957	W.B. Franklin	P.C. Bull	C.G. Gardner	Vice-Admiral J.S.C. Salter	G. Bracewell-Smith
1958	P.C. Bull	C.G. Gardner	E.T.W. Dodd	Rt. Hon. Lord Moynihan	P.E.M. Shaw
1959	C.G. Gardner	E.T.W. Dodd	R.S. Blundell	J.G. Carr	M.O. Sheffield
1960	E.T.W. Dodd	R.S. Blundell	Rev. A.W.G. Cope	R.E. Brook	Lt. Col. and Alderman Sir I.F. Bowater
1961	R.S. Blundell	Rev. A.W.G. Cope	Rt. Hon. Lord Moynihan	P.B. Powell	F.S. Bird
1962	Rev. A.W.G. Cope	Rt. Hon. Lord Moynihan	P.E.M. Shaw	G.T. Bentley	Col. and Alderman Sir Cullum Welch
1963	Rt. Hon. Lord Moynihan	P.E.M. Shaw	R.E. Brook	H.W. Wollaston	Vice-Admiral J.S.C. Salter
1964	P.E.M. Shaw and E.A. Last-Smith	R.E. Brook	Col. and Alderman Sir Cullum Welch	G. Bracewell-Smith	R.E. Liddiard
1965	R.E. Brook	Col. and Alderman Sir Cullum Welch	J.G. Carr	R.E. Liddiard	R. Wakeford
1966	Col. and Alderman Sir Cullum Welch	Lt. Col. and Alderman Sir I.F. Bowater	R.T. Hawes	R. Wakeford	Sir Richard Jenks

	Lt. Col. and Alderman Sir I.F. Bowater / Sir Gilbert Inglefield	R.T. Hawes	P.B. Powell	Sir Richard Jenks	F.H.W. Bedford
1967	Lt. Col. and Alderman Sir I.F. Bowater				
1968	R.T. Hawes	P.B. Powell	Vice-Admiral J.S.C. Salter	T.C.S. Cope	G.R.R. Brown
1969	P.B. Powell	Vice-Admiral J.S.C. Salter	G.T. Bentley	G.R.R. Brown	D.A.H. Sime
1970	Vice-Admiral J.S.C. Salter	G.T. Bentley	F.S. Bird	D.A.H. Sime	K.M. Leach
1971	Alderman Sir Gilbert Inglefield	F.S. Bird	G.R.R. Brown	K.M. Leach	Major-Gen. Sir John Bates
1972	F.S. Bird	G.R.R. Brown	H.W. Wollaston	Major-Gen. Sir John Bates	C.I. Bostock
1973	G.T. Bentley	H.W. Wollaston	D.A.H. Sime	H.C. Quitman	M.E. Bathurst
1974	H.W. Wollaston	D.A.H. Sime	Sir Guy Bracewell-Smith	W.A. Twiston-Davies	I.S.B. Crosse
1975	D.A.H. Sime	Sir Guy Bracewell-Smith	R.E. Liddiard	G.L. Bourne	J. Denza
1976	D.A.H. Sime	R.E. Liddiard	Major-Gen. Sir John Bates	M.W.D. Northcott	G.R. Fox
1977	R.E. Liddiard	Major-Gen. Sir John Bates	H.C. Quitman	M.A.B. Jenks	M.L. Hall
1978	Major-Gen. Sir John Bates	H.C. Quitman	M.E. Bathurst	P.C.F. Warren	J.R. Welch
1979	H.C. Quitman	M.E. Bathurst	W.A. Twiston-Davies	Sir John Welch	R.J.P. Jenks
1980	M.E. Bathurst	W.A. Twiston-Davies	I.S.B. Crosse	R.J.P. Jenks	B.E. Sturgess
1981	W.A. Twiston-Davies	I.S.B. Crosse	C.I. Bostock	B.E. Sturgess	A.D. Pilcher
1982	I.S.B. Crosse	C.I. Bostock	G.L. Bourne	O.M.W. Swingland	D.G.C. Inglefield
1983	C.I. Bostock	G.L. Bourne	M.W.D. Northcott	D.G.C. Inglefield	P.W. Bedford
1984	G.L. Bourne	M.W.D. Northcott	G.R. Fox	P.W. Bedford	B.E. Shawcross
1985	M.W.D. Northcott	G.R. Fox	O.M.W. Swingland	B.E. Shawcross	B.C. Gothard
1986	G.R. Fox	O.M.W. Swingland	M.A.B. Jenks	B.C. Gothard	M.D.G. Wheldon
1987	O.M.W. Swingland	M.A.B. Jenks	J. Denza	D.E.K. Eliott	N.K.S. Wills
1988	M.A.B. Jenks	Sir John Welch	B.E. Shawcross	N.K.S. Wills	H.N. Lund
1989	D.A.H. Sime	Sir John Welch	D.E.K. Elliott	H.N. Lund	The Hon. L.B. Hacking
1990	Sir John Welch	D.E.K. Elliott	P.W. Bedford	The Hon. L.B. Hacking	Dr C.J.T. Bateman
1991	D.E.K. Elliott	M.A.B. Jenks	B.E. Sturgess	A.R. Miller	J.E.G. Prevett
1992	M.A.B. Jenks	B.E. Sturgess	A.D. Pilcher	M.H.V. Jeans	M.R. Liddiard
1993	B.E. Sturgess	A.D. Pilcher	Dr C.J.T. Bateman	Alderman Sir Christopher Collett	M.R. Liddiard
1994	A.D. Pilcher	P.W. Bedford	D.G.C. Inglefield	R.H.M. Hamersley	T.W.A. Jackson-Stops
1995	P.W. Bedford	D.G.C. Inglefield	Dr C.J.T. Bateman	N.A.C. Branson	P.E. Davidson
1996	Dr C.J.T. Bateman	N.K.S. Wills	M.D.G. Wheldon	P.E. Davidson	G.M. Powell
1997	N.K.S. Wills	D.G.C. Inglefield	J.E.G. Prevett	G.M. Powell	J.E.N. Bates
1998	D.G.C. Inglefield	M.D.G. Wheldon	B.E. Shawcross	J.E.N. Bates	J.B.S. Swallow
1999	M.D.G. Wheldon	B.E. Shawcross	H.N. Lund	J.B.S. Swallow	G.F. Pulman
2000	B.E. Shawcross	H.N. Lund	The Hon. L.B. Hacking	G.F. Pulman	D.H. Juster
2001	H.N. Lund	The Hon. L.B. Hacking	J.E.G. Prevett	B.L.H.Powell	J.H.W. Hamilton
2002	The Hon. L.B. Hacking	J.E.G. Prevett	A.R. Miller	J.H.W. Hamilton	R.G.F. Glover
2003	J.E.G. Prevett	A.R. Miller	P.E. Davidson	R.G.F. Glover	J.W. Kinnimonth

List of Clerks and Beadles

Clerks

1931-1950   Guy Tryon Eagleton
1950-1966   Commander Harry Prevett, O.B.E., R.N.
1966-1983   Commander William Ronald Miller, O.B.E., R.N.
1983-1995   Captain Michael Ernest Barrow, D.S.O., R.N.
1995-2004   Captain Robert Julian Fisher, R.N.

Beadles

1934-1941   Lt Albert Raymond Hull
1941-1945   Harold William John Davis
1945-1968   Albert Edward Victor Hooke
1968-1992   Francis John Oakman, B.E.M.
1992-   Evan David Evans

Appendix Three

Retail Price Index, 1948-2002

As the text refers frequently to prices, the reader may find it helpful to have a reminder of the changing value of money. The following index of retail prices, taking 1948 as the base of 100 has been compiled from data available from the National Statistics government website: www.statistics.gov.uk. Interested readers may find the task of conversion easier by using the 'How Much is that Worth Today?' web site available from Economic History Services at: http://www. eh.net/hmit/ppowerbp. The site offers an easy means of comparing purchasing power from 1264 to 2002.

Year	Index	Year	Index
1948	100	1976	504
1949	103	1977	584
1950	106	1978	633
1951	116	1979	717
1952	126	1980	846
1953	130	1981	947
1954	132	1982	1028
1955	138	1983	1075
1956	145	1984	1129
1957	150	1985	1198
1958	155	1986	1238
1959	156	1987	1290
1960	158	1988	1353
1961	163	1989	1458
1962	170	1990	1597
1963	173	1991	1691
1964	179	1992	1753
1965	187	1993	1781
1966	195	1994	1824
1967	200	1995	1888
1968	209	1996	1933
1969	221	1997	1993
1970	234	1998	2060
1971	257	1999	2091
1972	275	2000	2153
1973	300	2001	2192
1974	348	2002	2229
1975	433		

Notes

1. The Company in the Second World War, pp. 1-16

1. CW, 1.6.1941; on the Blitz generally, see J. White, *London in the Twentieth Century: A City and its People* (London, 2001), pp. 38-40; S. Inwood, *A History of London* (London, 1998), pp. 801-04; City of London Corporation, *The City of London. A Record of Destruction and Survival* (London, 1951)
2. ESC, 7.1.1941
3. CW, 9.5.1941
4. CW, 4.2.1941; Wine Committee, 13.2.1941
5. FC, 27.10.1939
6. Corporate Accounts, 1945-1946; *A Manual for the Private Use of the Court of Assistants of the Haberdashers' Company* (privately printed, 1954, copy at Haberdashers' Hall), pp.16-19
7. ESC, 7.2.1941, 23.4.1941, 29.7.1941; SC, 26.8.1943; EC, 25.5.1944; CA, 11.10.1943, 22.11.1943, 13.12.1943
8. FC, 27.10.1939, 13.6.1940
9. FC, 4.2.1941, 30.9.1941; CA, 13.10.1941
10. CW, 19.9.1939, 7.11.1939, 6.2.1940, 2.4.1940, 4.6.1940, 4.2.1941; CA, 20.5.1940
11. CA, 9.12.1940
12. WC, 18.11.1941
13. SC, 28.11.1940, 5.10.1942; CA, 13.1.1941, 11.5.1942
14. SC, 24.2.1942; CW, 3.3.1942; CA, 9.3.1942, 11.5.1942
15. SC, 5.10.1942, CA, 28.10.1942
16. CA, 28.10.1942; OCC, 23.11.42
17. CA, 11.1.1943
18. CW, 1.1.1941; CW, 3.2.1942
19. SC, 1.4.1942; CW, 24.2.1942, 11.5.1942, 22.9.1942
20. CW, 3.10.1939, 10.6.1941, 16.9.1941, 4.7.1944; CA, 10.7.1944
21. CW, 1.10.1940; CA, 7.10.1940
22. CC, 23.1.1941
23. CW, 4.3.1941
24. CW, 4.2.1941, 4.3.1941
25. CW, 7.10.1941
26. CA, 12.5.1941
27. L.E. Ingarfield and M.B. Alexander, *Haberdashers' Aske's Hatcham Boys' School. A Short History* (privately published, 1985), p. 27; N. Goddard, *Reminiscences of a Headmaster. Aske's School, 1932-1961* (London, 1972), pp. 76ff.
28. H.R. Dulley, *The Haberdashers' Aske's School for Girls. The First 125 Years* (Oxford, 2000), pp.86-94
29. Goddard, *Reminiscences*, p.76; *Hatcham Tercentenary, 1690-1990* (Lewisham, 1990), pp. 56-64; Dulley, *Aske's Girls*, pp.92-3
30. Goddard, *Reminiscences*, pp. 76ff.
31. D. & R. Taylor, *Mr Adams' Free Grammar School* (Chichester, 2002), p. 145; H.A. Ward, *Monmouth School, 1614-1964. An Outline History* (privately published, 1964), p. 33; P. Rutter, *The Haberdashers' Oldest School. A History of the Aldersey School, Bunbury, 1594-1994* (privately published, 1993), pp. 136-8
32. EC, 2.10.1939

33. *Hatcham Tercentenary*, p. 49; EC, 2.10.1939
34. Goddard, *Reminiscences*, p. 119
35. Dulley, *Aske's Girls*, pp. 95-6; EC, 2.10.1939
36. ESC, 7.1.1941; CA, 19.11.1940
37. Ward, *Monmouth*, p. 33
38. ESC, 28.11.1940, 20.2.1941, 7.4.1941
39. EC, 15.10.1940
40. ESC, 7.1.1941
41. Inwood., *London,* pp. 804-08; N. Longmate, *Hitler's Rockets. The History of the V32* (London, 1985), pp. 207-16; L. Blake, *How We Went to War: Deptford and Lewisham, 1939-1945* (Lewisham, 1995); CW, 4.7.1944; EC, 23.1.1945
42. EC, 10.4.1940, 15.10.1940; FC, 16.11.1944
43. EC, 15.10.1940, 20.2.1941, 5.1.1943; Surveyor's Report on Kent estate in GL, MS 24722/2
44. EScC, 23.10.1941
45. EScC, 8.1.1942, 6.2.1942; EC, 4.3.1943; CA, 11.1.1943; FC, 4.5.1943; Dulley, *Aske's Girls*, pp. 96-7
46. FC, 27.10.1939, 18.1.1940
47. CA, 10.6.1940
48. CC, 23.1.1941; FC, 23.1.1941, 4.2.1941
49. CA, 14.7.1941
50. White, *London*, pp.40-1; Inwood, *London*, pp. 804-08
51. EC, 4.3.1943, 3.2.1944; CW, 2.1.1945
52. EC, 13.2.1944
53. EC, 3.2.1944, 16.3.1944, 23.1.1945, 8.3.1945
54. CA, 22.11.1943, 13.12.1943; EScC, 27.1.1944
55. D. Thom, 'The 1944 Education Act; the art of the possible', in H.L. Smith, ed., *War and Social Change: British Society in the Second World War* (Manchester, 1986); K. Jeffreys, 'R.A. Butler, the Board of Education and the 1944 Education Act', *History*, 69 (1984), pp. 415-31; Clarke, *Hope and Glory. Britain, 1900-1990* (London, 1996) pp. 283-5.
56. EScC, 25.10.1944; CA, 27.11.1944
57. Goddard, *Reminiscences*, pp. 6, 129-30; CW, 4.7.1944; EC, 23.1.1945

2. **Financial Transformations, pp. 17-38**

1. I.W. Archer, *The History of the Haberdashers' Company* (Chichester, 1991), pp. 71-88, 104-09, 117-19, 184; *Manual* (1954), pp. 21-5, 38-40, 44-6, 78-83, 90-7; J. Read, 'The Manor of Hatcham. Aspects of its Development, 1600-1900' (London Diploma for History thesis, 1973, copy in Lewisham Local Studies Library); R. Thatcher, *Hatcham and Telegraph Hill. An Historical Sketch* (Lewisham Local History Society, 1982)
2. FC, 14.3.1946; EC, 20.5.1946
3. EC, 30.9.1946, 1.5.1947, 4.2.1948, 25.2.1948, 1.4.1948; Hoxton Sub-committee, 13.7.1948
4. EC, 20.2.1947, 17.9.1947, 4.11.1947, 12.11.1947, 6.1.1948, 20.1.1948, 4.2.1948; FC, 15.2.1947; Metropolitan Borough of Deptford, Minutes of Proceedings, vol. 47, p. 433; vol. 48, pp. 145-6
5. CA, 11.1.1949; FC, 20.1.1949, 22.9.1949; EC, 26.5.1949
6. EC, 4.10.1948; FC, 22.9.1949
7. CA, 10.4.1951; EC, 11.4.1951; *Manual*, p. 40.
8. CA, 9.1.1951, 19.7.1955; EC, 23.1.1952; FC, 17.11.1954, 18.5.1955, 21.9.1955, 5.4.1956, 21.11.1956; *Manual*, p. 40.
9. EC, 11.4.1951, 6.6.1951, 11.7.1951, 22.10.1952; CW, 1.7.1952; FC, 20.7.1954
10. EC, 23.1.1952

11. Fourth Report of Hatcham Advisory Committee, 2.2.1956; Fifth Report of Hatcham Advisory Committee, 13.3.1957; FC, 5.4.1956; EC, 16.5.1956; CA, 12.2.1957

12. EC 80/1960, 83(ii)/1960, 93/1960, 105/1960; JMCC, 18/1961, 8/1964, 64/1965; CA, 14(d)/1962, 22(b)(ii)/1962

13. JMCC, 42/1964

14. JMCC, 32/1963, 18(b)(iii)/1964; CW 147/1964

15. HACC, 27/1963, 22(a)/1964, 47/1964

16. Fourth Report of Hatcham Advisory Committee, 2.2.1956; Fifth Report of Hatcham Advisory Committee, 13.3.1957; CA, 12.2.1957, 9.4.1957; FC, 12.7.1957, 4.12.1957; EC, 21/1958, 164/1958; JMAC, 4/1958, 15/1948, 2/1959; JMCC, 22/1963

17. JMCC, 43/1964, 50/1964

18. Report of Working Party appointed by JMCC, 22.4.1973

19. JMAC, 5/1958; CA, 107/1958

20. Hatcham Estate Select Committee, 19.4.1968

21. Report from Ritblat, in GL, MS 24722/2; AAAC, 16/1973; Joint meetings with AAAC, JMC, FEC, 29.6.1973, 31.7.1973, 14.9.1973; CA, 11(b)(i)/1974; FEC, 16.1974

22. P. Clarke, *Hope and Glory. Britain 1900-1990* (London, 1996), pp. 351-353; CA, 51(b)/1975; interview with Harold Quitman

23. CA, 39(b)/1979; interviews with Harold Quitman, Christopher Bostock, Michael Barrow, and Keith Way

24. PC, 256/1984

25. PC, 164/1983, 222/1983; CA, 43(b)/1983, 52(b)(iii)/1983

26. PC, 254/1984, 75/1985; FC, 6/1986; CA, 69(b)(i)/1991

27. PC, 98/1991, 161/1991, 222/1991; CA, 52(b)(i)/1991, 60(b)(ii)/1991

28. CA, 69(b)(i)/1991; PC, 115/1991; CA, 2(b)(ii)/1993; CW, 143/1993

29. CA, 65(b)(i)/1993

30. CA, 90(b)/1983; CW, 219/1994

31. CA, 39(b)/1979, 49(b)(i)/1979, 70(c)/1985; CC, 103/1979; PC, 68/1986, 73/1986, 127/1986; interview with Keith Way

32. FC, 6/1986, 26/1988; PC, 3/1987, 61/1987, 69/1987

33. PC, 69/1987; CW, 163/1990, 171(c)/1990

34. FC, 19/1997; CA, 33(b)/1997, 59/1997, 90(b)(i)/1997; PC, 40/1997

35. FEC, 20/1972, 41/1972; AACC, 54/1972; CA, 50(b)(i)/1972, 105(b)(i)/1973

36. JMCC, 136/1980, 149/1980, 160/1980, 2/1981, 9/1981; CA, 89(b)/1980, 32/1981, 42/1981; CW, 131/1982

37. Data supplied by Christopher Bostock

38. Data supplied by Christopher Bostock

39. Corporate Accounts, 1949-1950, 2000-2001; *Manual*, pp. 16-19.

40. EC, 24.3.1954, 28.4.1954, 15.9.1954, 20.10.1954; FC, 13.7.1955

41. CA, 11.10.1948, 12.7.1949, 26.9.1949, 11.10.1949, 13.5.1951, 11.12.1951, 21.4.1954, 13.7.1954, 21.9.1954, 19.10.1954, 14.12.1954; EC, 18.10.1949; FC, 21.2.1950, 26.9.1950, 13.7.1955, 4.12.1957

42. CA, 66(b)(i)/1972

43. CW, 16.11.1955; CA, 13.12.1955

44. Interviews with Harold Quitman and Keith Way; CW,116(b)(ii)/1978; PC, 265/1981, 269/1981; CW, 147/1981, 9/1982, 143/1982; CA, 58(b)(i)/1981

45. CA, 66(b)(i)/1972; FEC, 30/1972, 35(b)/1972, 40(i)/1972, 3/1973, 12(a)/1973, 21/1973

46. Interview with Harold Quitman; CA5/1976, 78/1976, 64(b)(i)/1977, 79(b)(i)/1977, 82(b)(i)/1977

47. CA, 40(b)(v)/1964, 64(b)(ii)/1964; CW, 37/1969; CA, 38/1969

48. CW, 168/1969

49. CA, 77/1975, 115/1975

50. CA, 22/1983; CW, 80/1983

51. PC, 50(b)/1990, CA, 14(b)(i)/1990, 64(b)/1990; Corporate Accounts, 1994-1995; for more on Garrard House and the Hall, see ch. 7
52. CA, 71(b)(i)/1992
53. PC, 9/1992; FC, 18(b)/1992, 23/1994; CA, 47(b)(ii)/1992, 71(b)(i)/1992, 83(b)(i)/1992, 120(b)(i)/1992; CA, 8(b)/1993 43(b)(i)/1993; 27(b)(i)/1994, 48(c)(i)/1994, 57(b)(i)/1994, 68(b)(i)/1994; CW, 23/1995
54. CA, 20(b)(i)/2000, 60(b)(i)/2000
55. CA, 44(b)(ii)/1996
56. CA, 45(a)(i)/1998
57. CA, 132(b)/2000; *Master's Newsletter*, 2002; see also below, ch.7
58. Data supplied by Christopher Bostock
59. This analysis owes a great deal to Christopher Bostock.
60. FC4/1994; CA, 96(b)(ii)/1994, 4/1995, 8(b)(i)/1995, 16(b)(i)/1995, 90(i)/1996; CW, 156/1997; interview with Michael Kerrigan
61. Interview with Michael Kerrigan

3. The Organisation of the Company, pp. 39-60
1. Archer, *Haberdashers*, pp.160-4; *Manual* (1954), p. 10
2. Planning Committee, 1.5.1947; 500th Anniversary Committee, 18.9.1947
3. Analysis of meetings from minute books
4. CA, 70/1958, 87/1958, 19(b)(ii)/1961, 75/1961, 79(b)/1961
5. CA, 42(b)(ii)/1968, 47(b)/1968, 9(b)(i)/1969
6. CW, 130/1972; CA, 69(b)(vi)/1972
7. CW, 60/80; CA, 98(b)/1980
8. CW, 89/1981
9. CW, 131/1982, 65(b)(iv)/1982; FC, 14/1986
10. CW, 241/1988, 75/1989, 90/1989, 103(c)/1989; CA, 32(b)(iii)/1989, 96/1989
11. Corporate Review, 1999; CW, 145/1998, 205/1998; interviews with Brian Shawcross, Sir John Welch, and Sir Brian Jenks
12. CA, 14.2.1950, 18.4.1950
13. CA, 40(b)(v)/1964, 64(b)(iii)/1964
14. CA, 35/1969, 59(b)(iii)/1969; CW, 161/1969
15. Corporate Review, 1999
16. CA83(b)(ii)/1984; Corporate Review, 1984
17. CA, 97(b)(iv)/1984
18. JMCC46(a)/1972, 66/1972; SC8/1972, 1/1973; CW, 199/1992; CA, 74/1993
19. CA, 15(b)(i)/1982; CW, 50(ii)/1982, 183(b)/1994
20. CW, 172/1979
21. Interviews with David Sime and Christopher Bostock. Note that in 1961 the Wine Committee agreed that vintage port should not normally served at lunch, save on the occasion of meetings of the Courts of Wardens and Assistants: Wine Committee, 17.7.1961. For the wider context of changing patterns of City sociability, see D. Kynaston, *The City of London. A Club No More, 1945-2000* (2001).
22. CW, 64/1969; CA, 21(b)(i)/1969, 33(b)/1969
23. CW, 112/1983; CA48(b)(iv)/1969, 53(b)(v)/1983
24. Corporate Review, 1999
25. Standing Orders Committee Report, 1952, filed in GL, MS 24722/2
26. CA, 70/1958, 87/1958, 32/1964
27. CW, 19/1961
28. Interview with Michael Barrow
29. Corporate Review, 1999; interview with Sir John Welch
30. Interview with Michael Barrow

31. Analysis based on printed lists of members; biographies of those holding high office in *Company Newsletters*, 1997-2002

32. *The Times*, 5.11.1998; *The Independent*, 19.11.1998

33. *The Times*, 15.10.1991; *The Independent*, 25.11.1991

34. *The Times*, 1.2.1992

35. CA, 9.4.1957; CA, 154/1963; Kynaston, *A Club No More*, pp. 40-1, 476-8.

36. GL, MS 24722/2 for the report of the committee on standing orders; CA, 70/1958, 87/1958; interview with David Sime

37. CW, 91/1989, 198/1989; CA, 40(b)(ii)/1989; Corporate Review, 1999; interviews with David Sime and Sir John Welch

38. Corporate Review, 1999

39. Interviews with Sir Brian Jenks and Michael Barrow

40. CA, 10.12.1957. The refrain may induce a certain scepticism about whether burdens actually increased!

41. This and the paragraph following draw upon the diary and scrapbook of Brian Shawcross, Master in 2000-2001

42. The selection of men named in this paragraph reflects those named as most influential in the Company's affairs by interviewees.

43. Interview with Michael Barrow

44. Information provided by Julien Prevett

45. Information provided by Michael Barrow

46. Information provided by Michael Barrow

47. Newsletter, 1995

48. CA, 14.6.1949; Reorganisation Committee, 24.5.1950, 5.7.1950

49. CW, 151/1982, 51/1983

50. CA74/93, 146/1998; http://www.haberdashers.co.uk

51. Details of staff in Confidential Minute Book amplified by information from Michael Barrow. I have deliberately not recorded details of salaries for the later period.

52. The environmental study is contained in GL, MS 24722/2

53. CW, 37/73

54. This section continues to draw upon the Confidential Minute Book, together with information from recent and current members of staff.

55. CW, 138/84; interview with John Cope.

56. Interviews with Michael Barrow and David Evans

57. Names of professional advisers are recorded at the beginning of each Haberdasher year in the minute books. For Dawsons, see CA, 11.4.1950

58. Reorganisation Committee, 24.5.1950, 5.7.1950, 21.9.1950

59. CA, 14(e)/1962

60. CA, 47(b)(i)/1962, 5(b)/1963, 168(b)(iii)/1963

61. CA, 75(b)(i)/1963; CW, 95/1963

62. Interview with Michael Barrow

63. CA, 54(b)(i)/1978, 61(b)(iv)/1978; interviews with Harold Quitman, Christopher Maunder-Taylor, and Keith Way

4. The Company and its Members, pp. 61-88

1. Archer, *Haberdashers*, pp. 96-7, 167

2. Interviews with David Sime, Gordon Bourne, and Harold Quitman

3. Interview with Michael Barrow; CW, 139/1976

4. *The City Press*, 24.5.1946; *Who was Who*; *Who's Who*; interview with Sir Brian Jenks

5. Interview with John Cope

6. CA, 110/1998

7. CW, 100/1963

8. CW, 58/1988, 255/1989

9. CW17/1961, 100/1963, 117/1963
10. Report of sub-committee on entry into the Company, 14.1.1969, CA, 21(b)(i)/1969
11. Freedom Register
12. CA, 6/1972
13. *List of Members*, 2000
14. *Lists of Members* for 1933, 1990, 1998. On schools staff, see CA, 8/1980; CW, 36/1986
15. Interviews with David Sime, Gordon Bourne, and Michael Barrow; CA, 79(b)(i)/1986; CW, 159/1986, 243/1988
16. CW, 7.11.1944
17. Freedom Registers
18. CA, 100/1972; CW, 88/1972, 84/1987
19. *List of Members*; Freedom Register
20. Interview with Brian Shawcross
21. CW, 89/1986; CA, 31(b)(ii)/1986
22. CW, 16(b)(i)/1989
23. CW, 73/1993; CA, 9(b)(i)/1993, 29(b)(v)/1993
24. CW, 41/1998, 63/1998, 105(b)/1998, 146/1998; CA, 29(b)(vi)/1998, 46(b)(vii)/1998, 109(b)(iii)/1998, 110/1998, 129(b)(ii)/1998
25. CA, 110/1998
26. CW, 191(a)/1998; CA, 6(b)(iii)/1999, 20(b)(i)/1999, 99/1999; *Master's Newsletter*, 1999
27. *The City Press*, 21.6.1946; CW, 1.1.1946, 7.1.1947
28. CA, 14.7.1947, 9.2.1948, 14.6.1948, 15.7.1948, 11.10.1948; 500th Anniversary Committee, 18.9.1947, 19.2.1948, 24.3.1948
29. CW, 5.4.1949, 1.11.1949, 7.12.1949, 5.12.1950; FC, 5.4.1949; CA, 11.4.1949
30. CW, 3.1.1950, 2.5.1950, 5.3.1951, 3.4.1951, 1.5.1951, 3.6.1951, 3.7.1951, 18.9.1951; FC, 16.3.1950, 4.4.1950; CA, 26.9.1949, 18.4.1950, 9.5.1950, 13.2.1951, 13.3.1951, 12.2.1952, 11.3.1952
31. CW, 7.7.1953, 5.5.1953, 4.6.1953, 8.9.1953; CA, 16.6.1953
32. CW, 4.11.1952, 6.1.1953, 3.3.1953; CA, 13.1.1953, 10.2.1953, 15.9.1953; interview with Christopher Bostock
33. CW, 2.3.1954, 4.5.1954, 1.2.1955, 1.3.1955; CA, 8.2.1955, 21.6.1955
34. CA, 13.3.1956, 10.4.1956, 9.5.1956; Papers on opening of Hall, GL, MS 24722/2
35. CW, 5.2.1957; CA, 12.2.1957, 18/1958, 6(b)/1959, 16(b)/1959, 134(b)(i)/1959
36. CW, 29/1961; CA, 5(b)(i)/1961
37. CW, 135/1962; CA, 113(b)(iii)/1962
38. Scrapbook of menus; CW, 10/1964, 91/1967, 121/1967
39. CW, 79/1965
40. House Committee, 9.11.1948
41. Prevett's letter is filed in GL, MS24722/2. Sir Lindsay Ring was the Lord Mayor who served scampi at the Lord Mayor's Banquet. *The Times*, 11.9.1997.
42. CW, 36/1984
43. CW, 123/1990; CA, 3(b)(ii)/1990
44. CW, 41/1992
45. CA, 23(b)/1974
46. CA, 51/1989, 70(b)(i)/1994, 11(b)(ii)/1998
47. Reports on wine consumption in GL, MS 24722/2; Wine Committee, 2.5.1985
48. Above, n.27; House Committee, 25.11.1949; CA, 10.11.1954, 69(b)(v)/1972, 89/1975
49. CW, 2.5.1947; CA, 71(b)/1970, 16(b)(iv)/1982; interviews with Michael Barrow and Christopher Bostock
50. CW, 7/1961; CA, 5(b)(i)/1961, 53/1964
51. CA, 104(b)/1968, 66/1971
52. Menu card in album of miscellaneous cuttings, menus etc.
53. CW, 167/1970, 152/1981, 169/1981

54. CA, 22(b)(iii)/1971; CW, 61/1972, 66/1972
55. CW, 41/1976, 55/1981, 190/1981, 101/1996, 207/1996
56. CW, 218/1984; interview with Michael Barrow
57. CW, 218/1984, 55/1985, 133(d)/1985
58. CW, 91/1993; CA, 58/94. After her martryrdom, St Catherine was transported by angels to Mount Sinai, where the Orthodox monastery now stands.
59. CW, 183/1985, 200/1986, 170/1988, 221/1988, 238(c)/1989, 202/1990, 111/1992, 135/1992, 194/1994, 155/1995; interview with Michael Barrow
60. Interview with Michael Barrow
61. CW, 150 (c)/1987, 22/1988, 16/1990
62. CW, 142/1985, 29/1994, 38(d)/1994, 84(a)/1994
63. CW, 4(f)/1995, 182/1995, 61/1997
64. CW, 9/1997 summarises events open to Liverymen and freemen; cf. CW, 100/1997
65. CA, 87/2000
66. CA, 10.3.1947, 8.12.1947
67. CW, 28/1987; 42(c)/1987; CA, 14(b)(iii)/1987
68. CW, 49/1967, 111/1967, 106/1981, 59(b)(ii)/1984; 116/1984; CA, 64(b)(iv)/1977, 18(b)(v)/1981, 34/1982, 92/1982, 17/1985
69. *Monmouthshire Beacon*, 14.6.1957; *Willesden Chronicle*, 2.8.1957; CW, 63/1961
70. CW, 17.9.1957; CA, 40(b)(i)/1960
71. Archer, *Haberdashers*, pp. 283-284
72. CA, 29(b)(ii)/1966; CW, 113/1974
73. *Who was Who*; *Who's Who*; CA, 55/1959; CW, 65(b)(iii)/1992, 143(b)/1992, 215/1994
74. CW, 91/1980, 138/1980, 68/1992
75. CA, 45(b)/1973
76. Below, pp. 125-6
77. CA, 87/2000
78. *Country Life*, 28.11.1947; CA, 13.10.1947, 24.11.1947; CW, 134/1963, 142/1981
79. CW, 74/1980, 139/1980, 62/1992
80. CA, 4(b)/1977, 17/1977, 23(b)(iii)/1977, 52(b)/1977
81. *Master's Newsletter*, 2002
82. Archer, *Haberdashers*, pp. 176, 177, 200, 215, 216; *DNB*
83. CA, 21.9.1954, 10.11.1954; CW, 4.1.1955, 1.2.1955; CA, 33(b)(i)/1966, 70/1966
84. Something of the variety of Princess Margaret's commitments can be seen from the following schedule of visits between 1967 and 1979: Acton Girls (1967), Albrighton (1968), Elstree Boys (1969), Hatcham (1970), Bunbury (1972), Hatcham (1973), Elstree Girls (1974), Hatcham (1975), Monmouth (1976), meeting of Minor Charities Committee (1978), Hatcham (1979): CA, 41/1967; CW, 108/1968, 12/1969; CA, 30/1971, 27/1972, 68/1973, 52/1974, 9/1975, 84(b)(i)/1976, 3(b)(ii)/1978, 1/1979. There were no visits in 1977 because of the Silver Jubilee: CA, 21/1977
85. CA, 194(b)/1984
86. CW, 89/1986: CA, 31(b)(ii)/1986
87. Interview with David Sime
88. CW, 2.5.1944, 2.1.1945, 16.2.1945, 1.5.1945, 5.6.1945, 6.11.1945
89. *DNB*
90. *DNB*
91. *Who was Who*; information from Julien Prevett
92. CW, 79/1958, 140(f)/1994; CA, 78/1967, 48(b)(iii)/1969, 63/1969; CW, 163/1980
93. Archer, *Haberdashers*, pp. 216-217; CW, 83/1961. Michael Barrow has been helpful on the service affiliations.
94. CW, 103/1983; CA, 19(b)(iv)/1984; CW, 53/1992
95. CW, 206/1986; *Master's Newsletter*, 2002
96. CW, 163/1991; *Master's Newsletter*, 1992

97. *Master's Newsletter*, 1994
98. CW, 15/1988, 4(e)/1996; CA, 64(b)(iv)/1990, 34/1991; *Master's Newsletter*, 1997
99. CW, 39(b)/1989, 50(e)/1989; *Master's Newsletter*, 2002
100. CW, 164/1977, 52/1993; CA, 50(b)(i)/1999
101. *The Sphere*, 13.10.1956
102. CW, 23/1958, 85/1958, 112/1958, 60/1960, 98/1961
103. CW, 63/1984; *Master's Newsletter*, 2000; *Debrett's People of Today*
104. CW, 62(b)/1992, 52/1993; CA, 129/1997; *Voting for a World Class City* (Corporation of London, 2002)
105. CW, 21/1963, 201/1964, 159/1970, 191/1994
106. CA, 8/1965; CW, 75/1965, 113/1969, 172/1969; Minutes of Masters, Prime Wardens and Clerks, 9.6.1969
107. CW, 47/1980, 74/1980, 114/1980
108. CW, 182/1985
109. CW, 12/1958, 62/1969
110. CW, 76/1959, 180/1965, 189/1966, 19/1968
111. CW, 94/1991, 28/1992
112. CW, 148/1988, 41/1989

5. The Company's Charities, pp. 89-104
1. Archer, *Haberdashers*, pp. 71-88, 104-08
2. Charity Accounts, Aske, Jones, and Adams, 1957-1958
3. Archer, *Haberdashers*, pp. 82, 111-12, 184, 234-5
4. Archer, *Haberdashers*, pp. 106-10, 188
5. *Manual* (1954), pp. 56, 62, 74-5, 122-5
6. Archer, *Haberdashers*, pp. 40-2, 47, 198-201
7. Archer, *Haberdashers*, pp. 202-04; *Manual* (1954), pp. 83-4, 86-8
8. Archer, *Haberdashers*, pp. 192-3; *Manual* (1954), pp. 31-2; Rutter, *Haberdashers' Oldest School*, ch. 8
9. Archer, *Haberdashers*, pp. 194-5, 201-02; *Manual* (1954), pp. 27-8; D. & R. Taylor, *Mr Adams' Free Grammar School*, ch. 8
10. *Manual* (1954), p. 62
11. *Manual* (1954), p. 67
12. FC, 7/1960; CA, 49/1974; CW, 108/1994
13. *Manual* (1954), pp. 99-102
14. Report on Jones' almshouse charity, 1952, in GL, MS 24722/2; *Manual* (1954), pp. 102-03; CC, 29.4.1953; FC, 9.7.1953
15. CA, 10.4.1956, 7(b)(i)/1959; EC, 22.12.1955; CC, 34/1959, 86/1960, 15/1962, 58/1963
16. Archer, *Haberdashers*, pp. 72, 76; *Manual* (1954), pp. 104-06
17. CC, 18.6.1952; CA, 1.3.1952, 12.5.1953
18. CA, 14.11.1956; 14.5.1957; Report on Golden Lectures in GL, MS 24722/2
19. CW, 99/1969
20. CW, 21/1975, 58/1975, 78/1975
21. CC, 169/1978; CA, 99(b)(ii)/1978
22. See also the press coverage for George Carey's Golden Lecture in 1992, 'Putting the fear of God into the City', *The Independent*, 5.6.1992; *The Times*, 5.6.1992
23. Archer, *Haberdashers*, pp. 41, 54, 72, 76, 94, 95, 282, 283-4
24. Interview with Brian Blair
25. *The Haberdashers' Charitable Foundations Manual* (2002)
26. *Manual* (1954), pp. 33-7; interview with Brian Blair
27. Interview with Brian Blair
28. CC, 46(f)/1970; CW, 111/1989; CA, 51(b)/1991; 47(b)/1993; 3(b)(ii)/1998, 111/1998; interviews with Anthony Miller and Michael Barrow

29. CA, 5/1985; 66(c)/1985; *Newsletter*, 2001
30. CW, 32/1995
31. Millennium Appeal Brochure
32. CW, 91/1998; CA, 46(b)(ii)/1998, 62(b)(ii)/1999, 109(b)(i)/1999, 112/1999
33. *Newsletters*, 1999-2201
34. *Manual* (1954), pp. 55-56; CC, 199/1986; CA, 81/1987
35. CC, 111/1987, 209(b)/1987; CA, 8/1987
36. CC, 199/1986, 111/1987, 140/1994, 198/1994, 18/1999; CA, 81/1987
37. CA, 77/1993; interview with Brian Blair
38. CC, 34/1998; *Master's Newsletter*, 2001
39. *Newsletters*, 1999-2001
40. *Newsletters*, 1999-2001
41. CW, 198/1992, 77/1994, 154/1994; CA, 92(b)(i)/1992, 81(b)(i)/1994
42. *The Haberdashers' Charitable Foundations Manual* (2002)
43. CC, 34/1998, 34/1999; CA, 143(b)(i)/2000
44. Data supplied by Brian Blair
45. Michael Kerrigan has been particularly helpful on the changing framework of charitable regulation. See also, press releases archived on Charity Commission website (http://www.charity-commission.gov.uk): 16.10.1995, 25.1.2000, 25.10.2000, 31.1.2001; and the Commission's publications, *CC61, Charity Accounts 2001: The Framework* (2000); *CC62, Charities SORP 2000: What Has Changed* (2000). The Charities Acts of 1992 (c. 41) and 1993 (c.10) can be found at http://www.gov.uk/acts.
46. The remarks in this paragraph are based on comparison of the Charity Committee minutes for the 1940s and 1990s, together with the almoners' reports incorporated in the Committee's papers.
47. CW, 91/1992

6. The Company's Schools, pp. 105-28

1. *Manual* (1954), pp. 88-9; Endowed Schools Committee, 19.10.1950, 31.5.1951; CA, 12, 12.1950, 11.12.1951, 14.12.1954
2. *Manual*, p. 42
3. D. & R. Taylor, *Mr Adams' Free Grammar School*, pp. 153-6. The proportion of the costs of improvements to voluntary aided schools borne by central government progressively increased to reach 85 per cent in the 1970s.
4. Rutter, *Haberdashers' Oldest School*, pp. 142-4.
5. *Manual*, pp. 28-29, 42.
6. Rutter, *Haberdashers' Oldest School*, pp. 139-42.
7. D. & R. Taylor, *Mr Adams' Free Grammar School*, pp. 155-7, 159-60, 167-9; *Manual*, pp. 25-7.
8. CA, 136(b)/2000; *Company Newsletter*, 2001
9. K. Kissack, *Monmouth School and Monmouth, 1614-1995* (Hereford, 1995), pp. 124-9.
10. CA, 8/1958, 26/1958: JMAC, 14/1958, 4/1959; FC, 52/1960; GL, MS 24722/2 for Prevett's correspondence; Kissack, *Monmouth School*, pp. 128-9.
11. Above, pp. 29-30.
12. CA, 16.3.1954, 69/1958
13. HAACAC, 6/1958, 7/1958; ACC, 15/1963; EC, 199/1958; CA, 153/1958, 18(b)(ii)/1960, 28 (b)/1961, 61/1961; Elstree Schools' Committee, 12/1960
14. HACC, 35/1963, 18/1964
15. CA, 54(b)/1963, 66(b)/1963; HACC, 5/1963
16. AACC, 13(a)/1970, 22/1970; AAAC, 64(a)/1973
17. HACC, 21/1963
18. AAAC, 53/1970; Dulley, *Aske's Girls*, pp. 123-4
19. AAAC, 7/1971, 6(a)/1972; JACC, 31(i)/1971, 46(a)/1971, 60/1971

20. AAAC, 33(ii)/1972; CW, 111(b)/1972; CA, 36(b)(ii)/1972, 56(b)/1973; see above, p. 31.
21. Clarke, *Hope and Glory*, pp. 285-6
22. Aske Charity Committee, 19.12.1961
23. CA, 47(b)(iii)/1962
24. CA, 155(b)(ii)/1963; 105(b)/1965
25. Clarke, *Hope and Glory*, pp. 285-6; M. Kogan, *The Politics of Education* (1990), p. 189
26. Clarke, *Hope and Glory*, pp. 286-7
27. HACC, Report on the financial aspects of the abandonment of direct grant status, 1969
28. AACC, 41/1970: CA, 74(b)/1970
29. SC, 5/1971, 1/1973
30. CA, 27/1975, 34/1975
31. M. O'Connor, *Secondary Education* (London, 1970), p. 73
32. AAAC, 68/1972, 2(b)/1973, 17(a)/1973
33. Ingarfield and Alexander, *Hatcham Boys'*, pp. 35-6; S. Maclure, *A History of Education in London, 1870-1990* (1990); interview with Graeme Walker; SC 8/1975: CA, 54/1980
34. D. & R. Taylor, *Mr Adams' Free Grammar School*, pp. 174-5. The Taylors offer a compelling account which I follow here and in subsequent paragraphs.
35. ibid., pp. 175-6
36. ibid., pp. 177-81
37. ibid., pp. 188-9
38. ibid., pp. 190-6
39. ibid., pp. 197-200
40. ibid., pp. 200-02
41. O'Connor, *Secondary Education*, pp. 42-6
42. Education Reform Act 1988 (c.40) at http://www.gov.uk/acts
43. O' Connor, *Secondary Education*, pp. 43-6
44. *The Economist*, 14.7.1990; *Financial Times*, 25.6.1990; *Hansard*, Written Answers, 6/7.3.1991
45. I have benefited from a reading of Christopher Bostock's account of the affair (copy at Haberdashers' Hall); *Hansard*, Written Answers, 6/7.3.1991 carries the key facts; see also *Times Educational Supplement*, 23.11.1990.
46. CA, 94(b)(i)/1996; *The Economist*, 25.4.1998
47. CA, 62(b)(ii)/2000, 97(i)/2000
48. CA, 109()a)/1996; EdC, 49/1997, 69/1997, 74/1997; interview with Anthony Miller
49. *Master's Newsletter*, 2001; interview with Brian Shawcross
50. Interviews with David Sime, Christopher Bostock, Michael Barrow; Goddard, *Reminiscences of a Headmaster*, pp. 7-8.
51. CW, 161/1985
52. CA, 68(b)(vi)/1980
53. Interview with Tim Marsh.
54. CW, 168/1988; CA, 45/1989; *Newsletter*, 2000
55. CA, 24(b)(ii)/1985, 55(b)(i)/1993, 78/1993, 96/1997
56. Interview with Tim Marsh
57. 500th Anniversary Celebrations Committee, 24.3.1968; CW, 2.10.1951; GL, MS 24772/2, documents on opening of Hall, 1956
58. CA, 6(b)(iii)/1965; CW, 64/1965
59. CW, 110/1976, 122/1976
60. CW, 199/1986, 144/1988, 171/1993; interview with Michael Barrow
61. Goddard, *Reminiscences of a Schoolmaster*, pp. 156-158; CA, 9/1989, 105/1990
62. CW, 93/1991, 145/1991, 82/1992
63. CA, 39/1994
64. Goddard, *Reminiscences of a Headmaster*, pp. 159-60
65. Dulley, *Aske's Girls'*, pp. 108, 115, 117, 123.

66. CA, 27(b)(ii)/1985; CW, 89/1985, 121/1985; 3(d)/1987; CA, 9/1996
67. Interview with Michael Barrow; *Newsletters*
68. Interview with Graeme Walker
69. CA, 76/2000
70. Interviews with Bruce McGowan and Graeme Walker
71. AAAC, 23/1974: D. & R. Taylor, *Mr Adams' Free Grammar School*, p. 178.
72. EdC, 49/1997, 74/1997; interview with Tim Marsh
73. Interviews with Brian Jenks and Tim Marsh
74. JMCC, 46/1969, 73/1969, 65/1970
75. CA, 24(b)(i)/1972
76. SC, 56/1985, 81/1985; CA, 61(b)/1985, 76(b)(i)/1985; interview with Bruce McGowan.
77. CA, 77(a)/1987, 98(i)/1987; SC, 63/1987, 91/1987; CW, 67/1988, 58/1989. For continuing concern about RI at the schools, see CA, 121(b)(i)/1992, 86(b)(ii)/1993, 3(b)/1996, 106(b)/1997; SC, 96/1993.
78. Interviews with Tim Marsh and Sir Brian Jenks.
79. CA, 165/1996; CW47/1997
80. CA, 54(c)/1998; information from Robert Fisher.

7. From Staining Lane to Smithfield: The Company's Halls, pp. 129-54

1. PgC, 1.5.1947, 4.12.1947, 2.11.1948, 24.2.1949, 18.5.1949; CA, 8.12.1947; EPC, 4.2.1948
2. PgC, 30.9.1947, 24.2.1949, 18.5.1949, 16.2.1950
3. PgC, 14.2.1952
4. PgC, 29.12.1949, 16.2.1950, 12.9.1950, 16.11.1950, 22.2.1951, 8.5.1951, 30.5.1951; CA, 11.7.1950; Reports on new Hall in GL, MS 24772/2
5. PgC, 24.7.1952, 29.10.1952, 19.3.1953, 4.2.1954
6. CA, 8.4.1952, 10.3.1953, 13.4.1955; PgC, 4.2.1953, 19.3.1953, 14.10.1954, 11.1.1955, 3.2.1955, 29.3.1955, 28.6.1955
7. Photo album relating to construction of Hall
8. Corporate Accounts; GL, MS 24772/2; S.Clements (ed.), *A Short History of the War Damages Commission, 1941-1946* (1962)
9. GL, MS 24772/2. There was more segregation in the 1956 entertainments than those for the new Hall in 2002. See above, p. 69.
10. CA, 26.9.1950
11. PgC, 30.5.1951, 6.7.1951, 14.10.1954, 3.2.1955, 26.4.1955
12. PgC, 11.1.1955, 28.6.1955
13. CA, 21.4.1954; Photo album of Staining Lane Hall; Commander Prevett's *Short History*, pp. 11-16 contains a good account of the post-war Hall.
14. PgC, 14.10.1954, 3.2.1955, 28.6.1955, 25.10.1955
15. CA, 18.1.1955, 10.5.1955; PgC, 11.1.1955, 25.7.1955, 14.10.1955
16. PgC, 5.5.1955, 25.10.1955
17. PgC, 25.5.1955, 25.11.1955; CA, 27.9.1955, 10.7.1956
18. PgC, 13.9.1955, 22.12.1955; CA, 20.6.1956; Prevett, *Short History*, pp. 11-16
19. CW, 4.10.1955, 6.12.1955; CA, 15.2.1956; Archer, *Haberdashers*, p. 272
20. CW, 88/1962, 56/1968
21. CW, 148/1964, 56/1968
22. CW, 40(b)(iii)/1968
23. CA, 33(b)(iii)/1966; CA, 92/1982, 70/1986
24. CA, 40(b)(i)/1982; CW, 73/1982, 86(ii)/1982, 94/1983, 58/1984, 207/1984
25. CA, 91(b)(ii)/1983
26. For the negotiations and their significance for corporate finance, see ch. 2. CW, 185/1982, 9/1983, 21/1983, 170(iv)/1983, 196(ii)/1983; CA, 91(b)(ii)/1983, 97(b)(i)/1983, 117(b)/1983
27. CW, 44(i)/1984, 66/1984; CA, 29(b)(i)/1984

28. CA, 84(b)/1986, 55/1987, 63/1987; CW, 117/1987; PC, 65/1987

29. CA, 119(a)/1987; interviews with Harold Quitman and Keith Way

30. CW, 65/1988, 63/1990; CA, 16(b)/1988, 23(iv)/1988, 65(b)(i)/1988, 8(b)/1989, 31(b)(ii)/1989, 93(c)/1989; PC, 39/1989, 172/1989

31. CA, 14(b)(i)/1990, 64(b)/1990; PC, 50(b)/1990; CW, 21(e)/1991, 30/1992

32. CA, 16(b)/1992, 23(b)(ii)/1992, 37(b)(ii)/1992, 71(b)(ii)/1992; PC, 8/1992, 51/1992; CW, 165/1993

33. CW, 206/1993, 127/1994, 132/1994, 212(b)/1995; PC, 100/1993; CA, 57(b)(ii)/1993, 10(b)(ii)/1994; Hall Cttee, 2/1995, 13/1995

34. CA, 41(b)(i)/1995, 51(b)(i)/1995, 64(b)/1995, 72(b)(i)/1995, 79(b)(i)/1995, 91(b)(ii)/1995, 12(b)(ii)/1996

35. As n. 33, supplemented by information from Keith Way; CA, 95(b)/1996; CW, 165/1997.

36. CW, 88(a)/1996; CA, 44(b)(ii)/1996

37. CW, 129(d)/1996; CA, 95(b)/1996

38. CA, 17/1997

39. CA, 79(b)(i)/1995, 110(b)(ii)/1995, 12(b)(ii)/1996, 42/1996, 136(c)/1996, 154(c)(iii)/1996, 14(b)(i)/1997

40. *Smithfield Conservation Area Character Survey* (Corporation of London, 1996)

41. CA, 77/1997; interview with Sir Brian Jenks

42. CW, 89(b)/1996; CA, 78(b)(i)/1996; 'A Knight to Remember', *Property Week Supplement*, Nov. 2001, pp. 4-9; http://www.hopkins.co.uk

43. CW, 30(b)(i)/1997

44. The account of the building of the new Hall owes a great deal to discussions with the Chairman of the Hall Project Team, Sir Brian Jenks.

45. CW, 88(b)(i)/1997; CA, 72/1997, 84-86/1997, 119(c)/1997, 70(b)/1998, 84/1998, 99/1998, 105(b)(i)/1998, 126(b)(ii)/1998. Bostock and Quitman were among the sceptics.

46. CA, 58/1996, 154(c)(iii)/1996, 77/1997

47. CA, 106 (c)(iv)/1997, 114(b)/1997, 134(c)/1997, 8/1998, 45(a)(ii)/1998, 53(b)/1998, 69(b)(iii)/1998, 97/1998, 98(ii)/1998, 107(b)(i)/1998

48. CA, 23/1999, 102(c)/1999, 122/1999, 20(b)(i)/2000, 38/2000, 53(b)(i)/2000, 60(b)(i)/2000

49. CA, 154(c)(iii)/1996, 84-86/1997

50. CA, 84-86/1997

51. CA, 119(c)/1997, 38/1999

52. CA, 150(b)(ii)/1999, 162/1999

53. CA, 37/2000, 117/2000

54. CA, 125/2000; *Master's Newsletter*, 2000

55. Information supplied by Michael Kerrigan. The donations to the 1956 Hall contributed 10 per cent of the costs of construction; at the millennium the proportion of construction costs covered by private donations was just over 4 per cent.

56. CA, 132(b)/2000

57. Interview with Sir Brian Jenks; CA, 132(b)/2000

58. Interviews with Sir Brian Jenks, Brian Shawcross, and Michael Wheldon.

59. *Newsletters*, 2001-2002

60. *The Times*, 8.6.2002; P. Fawcett, 'Guild Hall', *Architects' Journal*, 25.7.2002, pp. 27-31

61. I have received invaluable assistance from John Cope on the Hall's decoration and furnishings. The following paragraphs owe a great deal to information derived from him.

62. CA, 140(b)/2000

63. FAC, 8/1994, 24/1994, 3(b)/1995; CA, 61(b)(i)/1995. John Doyle (Livery, 1966), a Past President of the Royal Water Colourists' Society, has contributed paintings of several of the Company's livings. See FAC, 3(iv)/1998.

Index

References which relate to illustrations only are given in **bold**.

Key

1 Livery hall
2 Reception gallery
3 Luncheon room
4 Court room
5 Committee room
6 Main stair
7 Display room
8 Drawing room
9 Library
10 Master's flat
11 Beadle's flat
12 Clerk's flat
13 Servery
14 Wine bin

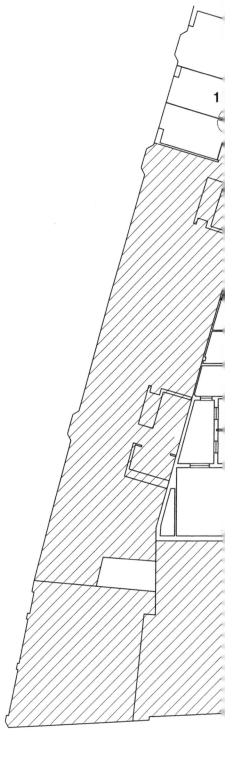

N

10m

HABERDASHERS' HALL
first floor plan Architects Michael Hopkins and Partners